# Embrace Your Story

## A Young Woman's Guide to Discover Who You Are, Where to Go, And Why You Matter

**Smith Minard**

For more information, email smithminard@gmail.com

ISBN: 979-8-89109-069-9 - paperback

ISBN: 979-8-89109-070-5 - ebook

## Get Your Free Reflection Journal!

As you go through the book, you will notice journal questions at the end of each chapter. To get the best experience, I've found readers who download and use the free Reflection Journal are able to implement faster and take the next steps needed to navigate changes in their lives.

## You can get a copy by visiting:

[https://tinyurl.com/freereflectionjournal](https://tinyurl.com/freereflectionjournal)

## Dedication

To the young women in my life whom I have the privilege of teaching, mentoring, and leading. It's an honor to do life with you. You each inspire me to live joyfully amidst an extremely ambiguous time in your lives. This book is for you!

# Table of Contents

# Foreword

## By Mary Spencer Veazey, Author

Change and growth happen all throughout our lives, but high school is a time where every limb feels like it's being pulled in a different direction. Do I do what I don't want to do for the sake of fitting in, or do I hold true to what I want for myself and risk being left behind?

I asked myself that question a million times in high school. The moments of trying to fit in felt nice but inauthentic, and the times of sticking to my gut and beliefs felt right but isolating.

Could there be a balance? I didn't know how to find one at the time. Juggling the world's expectations began to crash down around me and cover me in shame.

I hated high school, and I thought that going off to college would solve all of my problems. New people, new city, new everything. A fresh start is what I needed.

But here's the thing, every single place you go peer pressure and unrealistic expectations will follow. Hindsight's 20/20 and knowing what I know now, I wish I had a guiding hand or resource like this beautiful book you're about to read. You don't have to wait for a fresh start to live a fully abundant and joyful life. The life you're after can start today, in this very moment.

Maybe living fully alive and with purpose will mean you have to find new friends or set boundaries with social media or join a team or organization where you don't know a single soul. Be willing to lean into that. It's not comfortable, but the grass is greener where you water it. Plant those seeds and watch yourself bloom into the person God has created you to be.

When I went off to college and realized something was still missing from my life, I was at an all-time low. But I didn't want to stay there. So I started really pursuing a relationship with Jesus. I found a church family and a Bible study that I loved. I began asking one new stranger to lunch every week. I joined organizations I was passionate about and felt like I could contribute to.

And you know what happened? For the first time in a long time, I truly loved the life God had given me. Some lunches with strangers resulted in some of my greatest friendships. (Some of those strangers became my roommates years later, and I also was a bridesmaid in two of those strangers turned friends' weddings!)

I saw life for what it was: mine for the taking. God does not promise us an easy life, but He does promise us a life worth living. As you read through Smith's authentic words, she will give you the tools needed to discover what we're all searching for. As a high school teacher and Young Life leader for high schoolers, Smith is in the trenches with our high school friends. If anyone is equipped to speak into this topic, it's our friend Smith Minard.

The steps ahead are not easy, but they aren't complicated either. Don't let these words just be words; take action and I promise you will thank yourself later. High school feels so lonely, but we'll lock arms and get through this together. Smith is cheering you on, and so am I. A joyful life is just on the other side of all the chaos and brokenness. We can hold the brokenness and the beauty together. I pray *Embrace Your Story* leaves you better than you found it. I know that's what it did for me.

- Mary Spencer

# Introduction:
# Joy in Our Stories

All plants start as seeds. Seeds have everything they need to grow already; they just need to be in the right conditions. When the seed has everything it needs (water, sunlight, air, etc.), it "wakes up." Eventually, the seed grows a stem, the stem grows a bud, and the bud blooms into a flower.

I've found that we are a lot like seeds. We are waiting for the right things to click or our circumstances to change. Once we have the right conditions, we think we will magically become content in life.

Of course, achieving the "right" conditions is difficult, especially in this ever-changing world. But, no matter how much life is changing, the truth is we *can* put ourselves in the right places, right friendships, or right headspace to bloom. And then, just like seeds, we don't need to *do* anything to become flowers. After we receive love, care, and help, we have everything we need to simply flourish.

However, it's not always so easy. I'm sure we've all had moments where our lives suddenly feel different, and we find ourselves yearning for what once was. Life is full of transitions—we can't ignore them, and we most definitely can't get through life without having them. Young people are navigating dozens of daily changes: fake friends, where to go to college, who to date, breakups, what job to take, and identity crises, to name a few. It can all feel overwhelming, like we will never be okay, like life is impossible. How do you find the light and the water you need to flourish in times like these?

We just need a guidebook to find the sunlight and water we need to become who God created us to be: beautiful flowers.

*Embrace Your Story* has been designed to give you the tools and perspective needed to navigate life, one imperfect step at a time. Through the chapters in this book, you will find greater and more profound joy than you thought possible on the other side of change. This book is for young women who are confused about where to go next, who are unsure how to handle an unexpected life circumstance, or who desperately need to find some joy in their story.

## Why I Wrote This Book

As a high school teacher and mentor for many young people, I am on the ground with teenagers daily. I also lead high school girls through a really cool organization called Young Life, which helps kids know that they are seen, valued, and loved by God. I talk to young people every day. I see the comparison games, drama, friend group breakups, and unforgettable heroic moments.

I am truly "in the trenches."

Although I'm now in my mid-twenties, I still feel like I am on the cusp of becoming an adult. The struggles of college, job searching, and my first big breakups are still very fresh. I relate to and care about young people, and I believe that joy is for everyone, no matter how old you are and no matter what life throws at you.

I asked my students (thirteen to sixteen years old) to freewrite, responding to this question: "What do you wish adults knew about what it's like being your age right now?" No agenda, no grade. The answers were completely anonymous, and I had no intentions outside of genuinely wanting to *listen* to these young people. Here are the three things I heard over and over:

1.  Life as a young person is full of pressure. It can often feel overwhelming, and every day, it feels like there are a million expectations to live up to.

Here's what they said:

"I wish adults knew how much pressure kids put on themselves to be 'perfect.' The constant expectations of good grades while maintaining a balance between friends and sports is hard to live up to."

"We are held responsible as adults and are expected to be more mature and respectful like adults, but we are not given the freedom and independence that adults get."

"It's hard to live up to the expectations of older generations."

A lot of times, these expectations are coming from the very adults who claim to be helping and guiding them.

2. Even though adults were once middle schoolers and high schoolers, that doesn't mean they know what it's like to be that age at this moment in history. Empathy is required to truly listen without inserting our own experience.

"I know you guys were once my age, I'm not denying it, but you were NOT me."

"Being our age is completely different than when you were a kid. The anxiety you get by just walking into school is overwhelming. It can also be hard to be social because we lost that aspect of life for over two years (because of the COVID-19 pandemic). We really do try our best."

3. Being a teen has never been more challenging.

"I want [adults] to know that life is hard for us, even if it seems so much easier than yours. Gen Z has the highest depression rates, I think."

"I wish adults understood the difficulty nowadays with friend groups. There is an added difficulty of fake friends, group chats, and other technology. It is way too easy to just make a new group chat without a certain person without them even knowing."

"How can I be motivated to wake up and go to school, when I feel like I don't have close friends? We try to seem okay with everything, and at least for me, it works. Nobody really thinks something's wrong. Nobody really notices unless we talk about it, but that can be hard."

Life is full of change, and minute to minute, we can experience a range of emotions. I've learned that accepting that life is constantly fluctuating is the key. Life can be beautiful and enchanting and magical and also devastating and tragic and hopeless, for young people and for all of us. Accepting that is the first step.

## What You'll Get Out (And What You Need to Put In!)

In every chapter of this book, I hope to help answer the question: "How do you find joy in life's changes?" I plan to address those letters my students wrote me about the struggles of finding deep friendships, feeling misunderstood, and living up to others' expectations. I hope you enjoy the stories, see yourself in them, but most importantly, open your heart to the possibility of deep and abundant joy no matter what life throws you.

I won't be able to do this all for you, and at times, I will ask you to take some small steps yourself. I've provided journal prompts at the end of every chapter, and I urge you to journal anything that comes to mind when reading the chapters and answering the questions. This will help you process what you're learning and better implement the tools in this book. If journaling isn't your thing, reflect on the prompts while meditating or on a walk, or talk about them with a friend. Better yet, read this book alongside your friends or a mentor.

Finding joy might not be what you expect, and it requires more from you than you think. But don't be scared; I'll be with you every step of the way.

It's never too late to find joy in your story. It's never too late to take hold of your life. It's never too late to fall in love with yourself. It's never too late to be the kind of person that other people admire because your joy is palpable and overflowing. It's never too late to flourish.

We all need tools to navigate life, and we all need a place to discuss our challenges safely. I promise to give you a safe place to land, a guide to navigate what life throws at you, and the steps to take to live a life more joyful than you could imagine. Surprise: this book won't change what's going on in your life. But, it will change your perspective and thoughts, and grow your confidence and resilience to take on *anything* life throws at you. It might even change you along the way.

## JOURNAL IT OUT:

- What is it like to be you right now?
- What change are you experiencing in life right now?
- Who makes you feel the most like yourself?

# Chapter 1:
# Get Out of Your Comfort Zone

I had always loved running, but in college, I had the time and flexibility to finally take my exercise more seriously. It was nothing crazy, but I began consistently running around the lake on campus or going to the gym for a quick workout. Early sophomore year, one of my most disciplined friends trained and executed a half-marathon in Greenville, SC, our college town. It sounded fun to do that, too, so I spontaneously signed up for the Thanksgiving Half Marathon in Atlanta. All I had were a couple of months and some old running shoes. I found a running plan and got excited while writing out my cross-training workouts, paced runs, and long runs in my calendar.

While doing the half-marathon sounded *fun*, that isn't exactly the word I would use to describe the training process—at least, not for the first month or so. I don't wish chafing or shin splints on anyone, especially in the September South Carolina heat.

My parents told me they were separating in mid-September, two weeks after I began training. While it was devastating in many ways, I was thankful that I would soon return to my college campus. I didn't have to live in the middle of it. However, there I was, my mind a whirlwind of pain and fear, expected to run ten miles a week according to this stupid running plan I had created for myself. Running a lot of miles by myself, with my thoughts and fears swarming, seemed like the last thing I wanted to do those next few weeks.

But one day, it got easier. It was time for my eight-mile run in mid-October, my longest run yet. My pace was slow, but by mile six, my body was floating down the running path effortlessly. I was in awe, and praise was overflowing for the body God has given me. It was pure joy.

It was so powerful to slowly work toward something amid so much else in my life falling apart. How beautiful it was to create something new when something old was changing.

Running went from a daily chore to one of the sweetest times of my day. I made a rockin' playlist and started looking forward to my long runs. My body was no longer in pain at mile 6, but was instead invested in my prayer time, my "me" time, my gratitude time. Looking back, my half marathon training came at the perfect season of my life. God knew I needed space and time alone before I ever did.

The Thanksgiving Day race was approaching, and I was getting nervous. Could I really run 13.1 miles? Was I qualified enough for this? But there I was, driving to the start line. I tied my running shoes on a day that could have been filled with a lot of sadness and emptiness, a day that could have reminded me of the intact family I would soon no longer have. I started running with my headphones in, got in my groove, and never looked back.

On my first Thanksgiving with a changing family, I gained an accomplishment entirely outside my comfort zone. I experienced joy in the midst of suffering. It really is possible.

That Thanksgiving morning, I ran 13.1 miles in 2 hours and 20 minutes. I was proud of that. I didn't care about my mile pace; I barely even cared about those 13 miles. I cared way more about every mile before that, especially the moments before *that* when I decided to put on my running clothes and old running shoes and plant one foot after another on the same running trail.

I visualized my life as a building full of individual bricks, each one a unique moment of gratitude, answered prayers, sweet friendships, new creations, and visions coming to life. At times, bricks fall from our building because of things that are outside our control. We may lose bricks due to grief, unexpected circumstances, and loss. The more bricks we lose, the more we risk total collapse. This half-marathon was my way of adding bricks back into my foundation during a season where it felt like too many bricks were falling. Every mile I ran and every day I laced up my shoes were extra bricks. And that matters.

I left my comfort zone and tried something new during a significant life change. Running a half marathon came with an excellent reward: finishing the race. And while it was beautiful that I gained something amid loss, it was not about the accomplishment of finishing the race. It was really about the joy it brought me in that season when I so desperately needed some joy.

## Accountability Partner

When I was fifteen, my dad said he would take me on a trip to a Spanish-speaking country of my choice if I made straight A's in Spanish. My dad speaks Spanish, so he always shared the love of language with me growing up through his stories abroad and music. Every week my dad would check in, "How is Spanish class going? What are you learning?" I would gush about the topics and new words I was learning.

When I achieved the goal of making straight A's, I researched where I wanted to travel to and landed on Buenos Aires, Argentina. This would be my first trip to a Spanish-speaking country, and I was nervous and excited to use Spanish in real life.

Arriving in Buenos Aires was breathtaking and magical. The intricate and old buildings, smell of empanadas on every street corner, and the rumble of Spanish through both of my ears amazed me. I had never been anywhere like it. The most magical part of it all was that I got to experience it alongside my dad—my supporter and accountability buddy for traveling and speaking Spanish.

We took Spanish classes, met with his friends for dinner, and I grew more confident speaking in my broken Spanish. On that trip, we promised each other to always make traveling to Spanish-speaking countries a priority. A passion of both of ours—I knew that we would encourage each other to keep pursuing this interest.

Since then, we've traveled to six more Spanish-speaking countries. We have met new people, spoken our second language, tried new foods, and gotten lost on the twisted streets of Santiago, Chile. Throughout all of life's ups and downs–my awkward teenage years, transitioning to college, and setting out into my adult life–my dad and I have helped each other pursue our travel dreams.

I'm sure there will be many more adventures to come, with Dad by my side.

Finding people that inspire us to pursue our dreams and hobbies is crucial. When you're getting out of your comfort zone or prioritizing trying new things, find someone to join you in that.

It makes all the difference to share your dreams with someone else.

## Leaving it in the Past

Sometimes, getting out of your comfort zone looks like challenging yourself with a new activity, even if it doesn't end up being your new favorite thing forever. This is what happened when I joined a jazz guitar ensemble.

In third grade, I decided to pick up guitar lessons. My teacher, Jim, came to my house every Wednesday evening and taught me any song I wanted to play—I chose several by Green Day, Coldplay, and of course, the classic Taylor Swift. I loved it and genuinely looked forward to strumming and learning new chords.

In high school, Jim asked me to join the jazz guitar ensemble. As you know if you know anything about jazz, it is not the most accessible type of music to play on any instrument. In this group, we had to read intense sheet music and learn tough scales and chords. I was intimidated, and it challenged me immensely. We also met on Saturday mornings—let's just say my sixteen-year-old self did not want to drive to jazz ensemble on Saturday mornings. It got to the point where playing guitar was becoming more of a burden than a hobby that brought me joy. I wasn't delighting in it as I once was as a third-grader strumming Taylor Swift.

Stepping out of my comfort zone and joining jazz ensemble didn't work out exactly as I thought it would. Surprise: I'm not still playing jazz guitar. But I don't regret a moment of learning to play guitar. It humbled me, grew me as a person, and I'm at peace leaving it in the past.

I'm not saying anything that brings you stress or pressure is always bad. But for me, playing guitar—which once brought me great joy in an earlier season of my life—quickly turned into something that felt forced and stressful. We can all probably relate to this in one way or another: the subject that we used to love in school that became challenging at the Honors level or the sport we grew up loving that became overwhelming when trying to receive a scholarship to play in college. Sometimes leaving activities in the past is the best thing for us.

## Wrap-Up

Getting out of your comfort zone and trying something new can help you find joy in life's changes. It can bring great reward or simply make you happy, which is a reward in and of itself. Maybe I'm not running or playing guitar every day anymore. However, I can still be thankful for what those beautiful activities gave me when I was navigating transition in my life.

When your bricks are falling, start to build your own. Try something new, even if it's intimidating. Find something that lights your soul on fire. Do something you never thought you could do. Find someone you love to do it with. Maybe for you right now, this means simply getting out of bed in the morning and putting on real clothes. It may mean reaching out to one new friend, finally learning to cook with more than three ingredients, or trying that sport you've always wanted to try.

Remember, we don't need to commit to a lifetime of these things, but we can commit to a season of newfound joy. Let's create something new amid things falling apart. Let's feed our souls with capability. Let's tie our shoes, put our feet to the cement, and start creating the lives we want to live. Joy comes from building bricks while others are falling from your foundation.

## *JOURNAL IT OUT:*

- What have you been dying to try out?
- Who could join you or hold you accountable for trying this new thing?
  - Text that person right now!
- What is no longer bringing you joy that once did? Why?

# Chapter 2:
# Search for Redemption

Sometimes, life is just plain hard. Hobbies and traveling won't do the trick, and we need something a little bit deeper. This is what I felt like as I was going to one of my favorite events of the year, The Atlanta Boys Choir Christmas concert.

This yearly concert at Peachtree Road Methodist Church is magical and pure, and all things cheery and bright. There is nothing like hearing extremely talented youth sing every type of ancient and new Christmas carol to get you in your Holiday feels. Their perfect pitch echoes for minutes off the old church walls and windows. The twinkly lights fill every aching part of my soul. I lose my breath every time.

It was fitting that I met my mom's new boyfriend (now fiancé), Dick, at this event my first year going. Dick is a choir and music lover at heart, like myself. While we were listening to these voices, I got teary. This circumstance—my mother having a new boyfriend—wasn't exactly what I wanted, but redemption felt possible for the very first time. I enjoyed being there with him, and that was enough.

"Redemption" literally means "the deliverance from sin," or "the state of being redeemed," but I also see it as finding hope in unlikely circumstances. Little hints of light in the darkness. I never knew I could be okay in a changed family, but there I was, in that church, in awe of the redemption ringing with every note.

## Redemption Right Now

My therapist told me that people are inclined to dwell in either the past, present, or future. I had always been a "past" thinker, but I found myself living in the future during the divorce. The past had scary, dark holes I didn't want to be stuck in. The future had hope and possibility and a chance for redemption. My mind was constantly drifting to a future family of my own, a loving husband and happy kids that fulfilled all my dreams. Maybe that was my small, Southern school where "ring by spring" was common, or perhaps it was really what I wanted, but either way, I dreamed of a close, tight-knit family that enjoyed spending time together. I wanted us to be cuddled on the couch on holidays, playing card games, and going on vacations together.

Deep down, what I dreamed of was security, security I could only find in God. I wanted redemption for my earthly situation, and I knew my miracle-working God could provide that for me. I voiced this to my therapist and asked, since I felt it was my heart's desire, why wouldn't God give that to me?

She stopped me in my tracks with one question: "Do you really *not* believe in the possibility of redemption in your current family?"

In fact, I've always considered my family to be all of those things. We were close and enjoyed spending time together. We went on vacation and watched movies together on the couch. Even though things were hard right now, and circumstances were different, my family still had a rich and deep love for each other.

We were beginning to go on family vacations again, albeit with one parent missing. We were starting to laugh again, to enjoy mundane conversations around dinner. We were going on walks, and my brothers and I would drive together to the local pizza joint, the music up way too loud. Things didn't look the same, but I was still finding joy in the present moment.

Guilt often springs up when we feel joy in a situation that has also brought a lot of pain. For a time, whenever I felt happy for a moment with one of my parents, I immediately felt guilty because the other parent was not there to experience the joy with us. On Christmas, we started spending the morning with my mom, then drove midday to my uncle's house to be with my dad's side of the family. I enjoyed the special Christmas morning tradition, but Dad wasn't there with us. Being with my cousins on my dad's side was so much fun, but something felt wrong without Mom there. My mind would constantly drift to the missing person, like I wasn't allowed to have joy if my parents weren't happy, too.

New York Times bestselling author, Shauna Niequist, wrote it best in her book *I Guess I Haven't Learned That Yet*:

"...If you're in the midst of a painful season, don't feel guilty for catching yourself feeling happy every once in a while. That's not wrong. That's not betraying the loss. Let yourself be sad and then angry and then laugh really hard. Let yourself be tired and then anxious and then let yourself be surprised by a moment of beauty, of joy. This is how it is in the dark – confusing and circuitous and absolutely all the things sometimes, even in the same day."[1]

It took some time to learn that lesson, but suddenly there I was, in that church, letting myself feel pure joy from a situation I never thought I could. Finding redemption and joy right now, and not in the future. Allowing myself to feel happy and a bit sad at the loss and then an overwhelming sense of peace that God is holding me, and that it's okay to feel joy when things don't turn out as expected.

A year and a half later, Dick and my mom decided to visit me in Seattle on a cold April weekend. We ate at excellent new restaurants, drank a lot of coffee, hiked the Oyster Dome (and of course ate oysters after), went to some of my favorite parks, had a bonfire with my friends, and spent a lot of time with my now fiancé, Brian. Brian and Dick immediately got along, and we both loved spending time with them. We laughed a *lot,* prayed, and had rich conversations.

Redemption.

---

1  Shauna Niequist, "Waiting for Daylight," in I Guess I Haven't Learned That Yet: Discovering New Ways of Living When the Old Ways Stop Working (Grand Rapids, MI: Zondervan, 2022), 55.

## Wrap-Up

The divorce is not what I wanted, and the result is still sometimes painful. We don't know our futures. If you had told me five years ago that my mom and her new fiancé would be visiting me where I live in Seattle, I would have told you that you were absolutely insane. But that's how life goes, isn't it? We rarely expect it, and we always survive. More often than not, we find joy, too.

My life is not what I expected, but it is beautiful. This road I've been on has not been easy, but I look more like Jesus now. The path has been windy, but it's been forgiving, too.

Whatever situation you're in and whatever challenge you're facing, you'll be okay on the other side. It might take time, it might take work, and it will probably take a lot of tears. But there is great hope for redemption. And that redemption just might happen unexpectedly like mine did: during a boys' concert a few days before Christmas.

---

### JOURNAL IT OUT:

1. Write about one moment of joy from this past week.

2. Where have you seen redemption, hope in unlikely circumstances, in your life?

3. Is there any hope in the change you are experiencing right now? Any light in the darkness?

# Chapter 3:
# Cling to Others' Hope

You might be thinking at this point, "Is it really that easy? Just look for redemption, and you'll find it? This is not accounting for all the in-betweens and sad moments we experience. Come on, Smith, not every day is like a movie where we see light pouring into church buildings during Christmas concerts."

I hear you. I wish I could sit down with you and recount every hard night I went to bed crying. There are too many to count. My days are far from perfect; the majority are mundane and simple, and sometimes they are painful. This is when we need one of the most valuable tools in our toolkit: other people.

We are not meant to do this life by ourselves. Sometimes, we must cling to others' hope when we can't find our own. One day, we'll be able to repay the favor and be that anchor of hope for someone else.

In 10th grade, I didn't get asked to our school's Homecoming dance. I was definitely not the most popular, didn't find myself very pretty, and didn't feel confident around boys at all. It seemed like every other girl at school could easily flirt, apply mascara, and get every boy's attention, but I couldn't. I was hoping to be asked by *any* boy to the school dance. Alas, I wasn't, but something within me led me to rally a group of single girls to go out to dinner, get dressed up, and go to the dance anyway.

Looking back, I don't even remember that version of myself. Some courageous part of my 10th grade self sent the Evite to the other girls, made the dinner reservations, bought the dress, and danced the night away, even if awkwardly. Not having a date didn't stop us. There is power in finding hope in situations seemingly hopeless—and walking in with a group of girls was better (and easier) than walking in alone.

## A Text Message Full of Hope

During my parents' divorce, one text message helped me do the same: find hope in a seemingly hopeless situation thanks to a little help from some friends. We all have those special people in our lives who don't live near us. While we only see them every few years, they shape us immensely. For me, those people have always been my parents' Harvard Business School friends. While my dad was in business school in Boston, he became friends with four other guys from all over the country—California, Texas, New Jersey, a local Bostonian, and my dad, from Georgia. Through their friendship, their wives also became close friends through those two years. I was enthralled with story after story about their dinner parties, trips to Nantucket, and work events as they lived their early twenties together. It seemed straight out of the TV show *Friends*, and my parents actually seemed cool for once.

Eventually, they all spread out back to their hometowns. They kept up their friendship by going on annual trips, mainly to St. Simons Island in Georgia. And when kids were born, kids were brought along! We had instant friends from all over the country, with plenty to talk about since we only saw each other once every year. Those parents helped raise me—they were each so unique, different, and fun, and I looked forward to seeing them every year.

As most stories go, life gets crazy as kids get older. Travel sports, high school commitments, busy social schedules, and way less flexibility to pack up the families and meet somewhere across the country. We saw each other less and less, but our Harvard Business School friends continued to have a special place in my heart. When I got a text from Cindy, one of the moms, during my sophomore year of college, I didn't expect it. Cindy is the resident Boston mom but a Canadian at her roots. I could feel her calming and gentle spirit through the screen:

> "Hi Smith! I hope you are doing well...I am reaching out to tell you how sorry I am for you and your brothers about your Mom and Dad. You may not know this, but I was exactly your age when my parents decided to divorce. Even though I was kind of expecting it, I was pretty devastated. In some ways it was harder to cope with being on the cusp of adulthood myself. I know you have a lot of faith, and that will be a wonderful source of strength for you. I really wanted to let you know that having been through this myself, I am always available

as a shoulder for you to lean on. I would be happy to talk any time if you would find it helpful or reassuring. I believe I emerged stronger as a result of the divorce and it helped me with my marriage to Bill! I know we don't see each other very often, but I love both your parents, and you guys are very special to Bill and me. We had lots of good times together and will continue to in the future...I feel that it can be nice to talk to someone who knows the situation but is not involved in the day-to-day drama of it all. Anyways, just say the word and I will drop everything to chat with you. Sending you lots of love and prayers for strength. Cindy Xoxox"

I vividly remember reading that text outside a seminar classroom, with tears welling up in my eyes. I still get teary when I read it. I have never felt more seen than at that moment.

One of the most beautiful things in the world is using the pain and heartbreak you've experienced in your past to encourage others. Knowing I had a mother figure who understood what I was going through, praying for me and encouraging me from afar, brought me so much peace and joy. When I couldn't feel hope in my own story, Cindy encouraged me with a little text that her parents' divorce actually made her own marriage *stronger*. This is using our hardships for good, for change, for helping others.

## Young Life Camp

Fast forward five years later, and I am a Young Life leader in Seattle, Washington, taking high schoolers to camp in Malibu, Canada. After a bus ride, a ferry ride, another bus ride, and another boat ride, we arrived at camp giggly and excited for "the best week of our lives." Sienna, my co-leader, and I greeted our new girls in our cabin. We had never met them before but had been praying for them weeks in advance. I prayed that they could feel seen, known, and loved.

After five days of fun, adventure, and vulnerability, I learned that five out of eight girls in that cabin have divorced parents. I had never been more sure that God works on purpose. He intertwines our lives perfectly with the right people at the right times.

Because of my own experience with divorce, I was able to relate to these girls fully. Over the course of the week at camp, we told stories and opened up. I was able to empathize, counsel them, and understand their family lives from personal experience. This built trust in our relationships. Not only am I able to listen to their hurts, but I can truly understand their experiences. This allows me to love those girls even better than I could have before.

When you think about it, there's probably a connection we could find with every single person in our lives. Some part of their lives we could speak life into. We are all connected, an interweb of humans trying to make it through life. When genuinely interested in someone, we should find ways to relate to them, even when it might be on a topic we don't know much about. We don't have to lie and say that we love baseball and know every Yankees player on the lineup if we don't. But if a guy we are dating loves baseball, we could ask them who their favorite player is or bring up childhood memories of being at the baseball park with our families. Connection point.

Mac at the grocery store likes Georgia football, like I do. My coworker has a significant other she deeply cares about, like I do. A guy on my Young Life team is passionate about meeting kids where they are like I am. My student loves Mariners baseball way more than I do, but we can still connect over it and deepen our relationship through it.

The people I mentioned previously are different from me in *so* many ways. Even if we come from different worlds, we've found connection points, and now we can connect with each other, even if it's only over a game of football.

We look for ways to connect with those around us throughout our day-to-day lives without even realizing it. We make connections on highways when we see another license plate from our home state. We make small talk about how we both love potatoes in any form over a school lunch. We relate with girls at school by complimenting their hair or clothes. Without even realizing it, we are finding common ground with people to make them feel valued and have a sense of belonging. And they are doing it right back to us.

## Look for Someone One Step Ahead of You

The same thing rings true for deeper things. When we connect on a deeper level about something, like when we've been through a similarly challenging experience, we connect more intimately and can relate more fully. Cindy and I hadn't connected in years when she texted me that day. But, I felt seen, cared for, and loved by someone older than me who took the time to reach out. I felt hope that maybe, just maybe, I could use my family situation for good like she had.

We must lean onto people's perspectives that are one step ahead of us in their journeys. Their advice helps us push ourselves and grow. When someone's already been through the fire, they will teach us the best way to get out.

Think about it this way. I always tell the students on my tennis team that the only way to get better at tennis is by playing against people that are better than you. Play a level up, and you will eventually get to that level. We have to be okay with being worse and losing in order to improve. The same thing is true for learning Spanish. To get better at speaking a foreign language, we must speak with other people—especially people who know more of that language than we do. That's why they always say that complete immersion in another country is the best way to learn a language. We need input from others to grow. We need to be surrounded by people one step ahead in order to take that step ourselves.

Throughout my life, I am always asking: Who is one step ahead of me? Who is where I want to be? If I want to grow and find hope during my parents' divorce, I lean into the hope that Cindy's story provides. If I want to know if I will ever feel okay again after a breakup, I call up my friend who went through a devastating one last year. If I want to overcome my test-taking anxiety, I ask my teacher to connect me with an older student who has struggled with and overcome the same thing.

We don't always need other people's advice—sometimes, we just need their assurance that things will be okay. That I'll be okay on the other side of this, too. That we are taking the steps and finding the ways to grow and become better versions of ourselves every single day.

## Wrap-Up

The beauty is that *we* can be that "step ahead" for someone else, too. Just like how Cindy showed me hope with a single text message, I can now use my story to give hope to others—like you. Joy becomes tangible when we start viewing our stories not as hardships to overcome but as vehicles for change.

How do we find joy in life's most challenging moments? By clinging to others' hope when we can't find it for ourselves and then using our scars to empower others.

---

### *JOURNAL JT OUT:*

- Who is someone one step ahead of you and how might you ask for their help?
- Write about something you've been through that other people could relate to.
- What part of your story could be used for good?

---

# Chapter 4:
# Take the Next Best Step

I currently live in Seattle, WA, but I grew up across the country in Atlanta, GA. I always get the question: how did you end up here? Although I've probably answered that question a thousand times, I still stumble over my words.

I wanted something different. I wanted to live somewhere where I could go skiing. While I planned to go abroad, after I graduated college, the COVID-19 pandemic prevented me from doing so, so Seattle just…happened. Even more simply, this is where I got a job. While all of these answers are true, they don't fully answer the question: how did I end up here?

In my senior year of college, I navigated the ambiguity of what would come next. My friends were getting job offers and acceptance letters for grad school left and right, and I craved the stability and assurance of those options. I was a Spanish and Sociology major who loved people, learning, traveling, kids, writing, and teaching. I could become a Spanish Linguist, professor, or educational policy expert. I could go to law school and become a child advocate. I could totally switch paths and go into international affairs or business. I could move abroad and "experience my twenty-somethings," as social media urges us to do. I had no idea how to find my purpose. No clue how to figure out where I was supposed to be or who I was supposed to be.

There was absolutely no way I could pick one thing to do for the rest of my life. Instead, I tried to concentrate on the question: what is the right next step for me? This doesn't have to be my forever commitment to an office job, a teaching job, or a social work job, but simply a next step.

Although I could sometimes force this positive "next step" mindset, I admittedly had many hours of frantic job searching, LinkedIn applications, and phone conversations with every expert in every field. While none of this is terrible, it came not from a place of curiosity but from a place of fear.

How often do we execute tasks with good intentions out of fear and worry instead of interest and delight?

During that season of my senior year, my professors recommended that I apply for the Fulbright scholarship to teach English in a Spanish-speaking country. Fulbright has a "prestige" to its name and is well-known in the academia world for their goal to facilitate cultural exchange between the US and almost every other country on Earth. It is a government, fully-funded grant that allows the most accomplished US college grads a chance to live abroad.

This made perfect sense for me. I was a Spanish and Sociology major, had already lived abroad twice, made good grades, had an internship in D.C,...the list goes on. I am high-achieving and, to a fault, say "yes" to everything.

However, in moments of solitude, silent prayers with God, and conversations with friends, I knew I desired something different than Fulbright.

I craved moving to a new city, forming a deep community and potentially entering into a serious dating relationship, moving toward marriage and kids. I wanted to be somewhere I could *stay* if I wanted to, something more concrete than living abroad with an expiration date, again. I wouldn't get applauded for staying and wouldn't have the prestigious "Fulbright" on my resume, but my inner self was urging me to settle down, even as I was taking steps in the opposite direction.

As the story goes, of course, I didn't listen to my inner heart and applied to Fulbright anyway. I meticulously wrote my essays in October and interviewed three times before January. COVID-19 hit over my senior year spring break, I was shuffled back to my childhood home in Atlanta, GA, and the future was ominous and unknown.

In April, I got accepted as a Fulbright scholar in Colombia, South America. In May, the scholarship got canceled entirely.

A blur of emotion followed. Confusion. Devastation. Fear. But deep down in the hollows of my heart, I felt relieved. God literally had to shut doors for me so I could follow His best plan for me. I took two days to grieve the loss of what I thought my next year would be, then I spent hours applying for Spanish teaching jobs. Two weeks later, I accepted a teaching position in Seattle, a place I had never visited or thought of before. When I received the acceptance call from the school principal, I felt a deep rush of peace wash over me. I didn't know why, but I knew it was where I was meant to be. It was the next best step.

While little day-to-day decisions can be hard for me to make, the big ones come a bit more naturally to me for some reason. Where I want to eat, whether to work out or shower, whether to stay in, watch a movie, or go out—these are devastatingly hard decisions. Whether to move to Seattle, a place where I know zero people and have never been before, was a weirdly easy decision to make.

That June, after I accepted the job, my dad, brother, and I visited Seattle for the first time. As I was flying over Mt. Rainier, the never-ending lakes and water, and the green mountaintops that were still snowy on top, my heart felt settled. I had no idea what was in store for me in Seattle, but I could never have prepared my heart for the journey ahead: amazing community, tricky situations, a demanding but fulfilling job, loneliness, and falling in love. Little by little, my heart was softening to the simple truth that God's voice brings peace, even through discomfort.

I took the next best step. All I could do was hope that when I looked back, I would agree that I had chosen the path that brought peace to me and those around me. That I listened to God's voice, not the world's. That I took the right leap of faith, even when it seemed scary.

## Take the Next Best Step

Our entire society is built around "planning for the future." Every day, I meet with high schoolers who are panicked about their future—it's clear to me that we are creating anxiety in younger generations because of how we have set them up.

We send them so many mixed messages. Make a lot of money, but do something you are passionate about. Your twenties are for having fun, but don't forget to also find a husband and buy a house and have a kid by twenty-eight. Move abroad and live it up while you can, but if you're only starting your career at twenty-six, you'll be years behind your peers. Love other people and be kind, but also use people to get ahead, so you're on top. I could go on and on. We're taught what to do and what not to do, but the lessons all contradict and never really help.

When are we ever taught how to figure out what's *truly* best for our future?

When young people ask me how to know what to do with their lives, I try to teach them through what I have stumbled through: take the next best step for *you,* while keeping love in your heart for other people. I don't want it to sound self-centered, only saying "take the next step for *you.*" If we tend to make wild decisions, disregarding our family or closest friends' opinions, we should try to slow down and keep them in mind. I also want to avoid taking everyone else's opinions too seriously. It's a balance. We need to sit and contemplate what *we* truly want, while remaining conscious of others.

I try to boil it down to the one question, "What's the best next step?" You don't have to know the best step five years from now, but right now. Should I apply to this college? Would my first year in this career bring me experience and joy? Do I prefer marketing or art class? These simple questions don't have to bind our whole future, but they may help you determine whether your next planned step is actually your next *best* step. I still don't know what the next few years of my life will look like, but I can continue to take steps toward my ideal future life.

## Do You Want to See Him Again?

The "next step" philosophy can be explained well in the context of dating. I'm twenty-five, and I'm in a season where it seems like every person on my Instagram feed is announcing an engagement, marriage, pregnancy, or first home purchase. Dating is a hot topic in my friend circles, and although I'm no dating expert, I have plenty of horror stories and mistakes—which make for great advice I can pass along to others. Remember what I said before: learn from those who have been through it themselves.

I went on a first date a couple years ago. Before even going on the date, I was already sounding out his last name with my first name, imagining our wedding day. I know, I know—dramatic, much? I was jumping a hundred steps ahead and not taking the *next* best step. It turns out he ghosted me. So much for our wedding!

Instead of thinking about what could happen and what others might expect should happen, before even taking a moment to think: what do *I* want? Who do *I* want to be with? Instead of simply asking, "What's the next best step? Am I interested in seeing him another time, just for dinner?" I idealized my next twenty years and ended up disappointed.

My friends often ask me if they should continue dating a certain guy or end it. I always ask them, "Do you want to see him again?" That is the only important question right now. Yes, we should think about whether our values align with a prospective partner, if they are treating us kindly and respectfully, and if we laugh and have fun with them. Don't get me wrong here—there are a thousand important things to consider when committing to a relationship with someone. But, ladies, we don't need to know if he's our husband before date number three.

Do you want to see him again? If the answer is yes, the other answers will come with time. Take the next best step.

## Wrap-Up

Life is full of decisions. Some are easy, like, "What do I buy my mom for Christmas?" (who am I kidding, this is the hardest decision every year), and some are more complicated, like "What is my purpose in life?" or, "Who should I marry?" or, "What should my career be?" However, I've found that these big decisions are often solved by making many, much smaller decisions.

Over the past years, I've learned that being fearful of taking the wrong step will lead to being stagnant. Planning isn't bad, but sometimes option paralysis can sit in, and we will end up doing nothing—or making a choice for the wrong reasons. Taking a small step toward the future life you desire will lead to more and more steps in the *right* direction, even if you make some mistakes along the way.

I'm so thankful that I didn't say "no" to the teaching job in Seattle out of fear that I didn't want to be a teacher forever. It led me to where I am now. It led me to love, deep friendships, being around young people, and even writing this book. I said yes, not knowing exactly where it would take me but knowing that I was moving closer to the life I wanted.

You'll be okay wherever life takes you. Someone's been there before you. God prepared a seat for you. Jump in, take the next step, and—with one foot in front of the other—we will create something magical of ourselves.

## *JOURNAL IT OUT:*

- What is a decision you are trying to make right now, and why is it hard to decide?
- What kind of person do you want to be? Is this decision moving you toward that?
- What's one next step you could take? Can you make plans to take it?

# Chapter 5:
# Build Community

When I was getting ready to move to Seattle, I found my roommates on Facebook. Seriously, I did. Out of faith, I researched churches in Seattle, emailed their young adults' director or pastor, and asked if any girls in their twenties were looking for roommates. I was in awe of the generous responses. Pastors were connecting me with small groups and young adult Facebook groups. Young adults in churches offered to call me one-on-one to help me before my move. It is truly incredible what can come from a leap of faith, from reaching beyond your comfort zone. One girl I've never met put me in three Facebook groups full of young Christian adults in the Seattle area. I picked out a couple photos of myself and wrote a quick caption of who I was and what I was looking for in roommates.

People say that Seattle has the "Seattle Freeze," meaning Seattleites tend to give the cold shoulder to newcomers, only interested in sticking with the people they know and not opening their worlds to transplants. Turns out, there are plenty of young people in Seattle willing to open their doors to newcomers. I did a few Facetime calls with potential roommates, which felt like a mixture between interviews and first dates. I even had people reach out and say that they didn't need roommates but wanted friends, and would love to hang out when I moved out there.

I landed on a group of five girls who I felt were God's gift to me. Video messaging with them felt like talking to old friends, and I was assured that I would have built-in friends in a new city. One of them was even from Atlanta, twenty minutes away from me, and we had dozens of mutual friends. On my first visit to Seattle that June, we all went to dinner and chatted like old friends. My dad and brother started laughing; somehow, I had found immediate friends through Facebook.

Over the following months, we lived together, danced together, and watched *The Bachelorette* together. We cooked dinners together, threw themed parties together, and went through some really hard things together. We prayed, laughed, walked, played in the snow when the roads were shut down, and worked from home together. They let me into their worlds, introduced me to their friend groups, took me to their family homes, and exemplified Christ in their love and actions. I have now been to two of their weddings, and can call some of them my best friends to this day.

Taking a risk and emailing those churches led me to deep friendships in a foreign place. We never know where taking a chance to make friends can lead us. It doesn't always work out as my story did. I've had many failed attempts at finding real friends. But, sometimes, that one risk can change everything. I made a home for myself in Seattle because of those girls. And it all started with one email and one post in a Facebook group. The risk taken was not random; I was also positioning myself to live with people that had the same values and mission in life as me.

While I know that my community in Seattle was God-ordained in many ways, I was also intentionally doing two things: putting myself out there and aligning myself with people of the same values.

Although this scenario worked in my favor, I have had plenty of moments in life where I have felt lonely, isolated, and like I couldn't find my place, especially in my teen years. If you are a young person right now, you are not alone. You are passing hundreds of other peers in the hallway or campus feeling the same way as you: lonely and forgotten.

I was well-liked in ninth and tenth grade, but lived in the shadows. People were kind to me in class, and no one had a problem with me, but I didn't have any close friends. I had friends, to be sure, but none that would invite me to sleepovers regularly on the weekends. I was a friend-group "floater;" I didn't belong to one tight-knit group. In those years, I would go to the nurse's office and fake sick during the last period of the day on Fridays so my mom would come to pick me up. That way, I didn't have to deal with the anxiety of being around girls on a Friday afternoon who were grouped up, going to sleepovers or parties. I craved that sense of community, the sense of belonging, of being known in a group setting.

## Teens Lacking Community

Our entire worlds changed during the COVID-19 pandemic, which lasted quite a bit longer than expected. It's no surprise that loneliness affects young people more than anyone else, but we didn't know it would be quite this bad.

The Making Caring Common Project through the Harvard Graduate School of Education released the results of an online survey of approximately 950 Americans in October 2020.[2] According to results, 36% of all Americans feel "serious loneliness." 61% of those were young adults. Not only this, but 43% of young adults reported increases in loneliness since the outbreak of the COVID-19 pandemic.

When the study was released in October 2020, about half of the lonely young adults in the survey reported that no one in the past few weeks had "taken more than just a few minutes" to ask how they are doing in a way that made them feel like the person "genuinely cared."

Not only are young people feeling lonely, but according to the Adolescent Behaviors and Experiences Survey conducted by the CDC in June of 2020, 24.4% of teenagers reported that "their mental health was most of the time or always not good during the COVID-19 pandemic (poor mental health includes stress, anxiety, and depression)."[3] This is significantly higher than the same survey in 2019.

Is there any hope?

---

2  Richard Weissbourd et al., "Loneliness in America: How the Pandemic Has Deepened an Epidemic of Loneliness and What We Can Do About It," Making Caring Common, February 2021, https://mcc.gse.harvard. edu/reports/loneliness-in-america.

3  Mark É. Czeisler et al., "Mental Health, Substance Use, and Suicidal Ideation during the COVID-19 Pandemic — United States, June 24–30, 2020," MMWR. Morbidity and Mortality Weekly Report 69, no. 32 (2020): pp. 1049-1057, https://doi.org/10.15585/mmwr.mm6932a1.

In March 2015, Harvard's Center on the Developing Child released a study saying that every child who winds up doing well has had at least one stable and committed relationship with a supportive adult.[4]

That's the answer. We need people. And young people need at least one adult, who's not a parent, that takes an interest in and cares about them. One of my students who wrote me anonymous letters about what it's like being their age said, "I don't feel like talking to my parents; they don't listen or want to listen." This is when that trusted adult relationship becomes so valuable.

When one person—or better yet, a whole community—believes in us, it changes everything.

## Lonely at School

Not only are we seeing depression and anxiety levels rising at a national and international level, but I am seeing it in person with the young people I'm with every single day.

Two years ago, one of my students started her first year of high school online. In a time where she was supposed to be embarking on an exciting and new season of life, she was stuck at home, looking at classmates on a computer screen. She was lonely and isolated, without a single friend from school.

---

4 "Supportive Relationships and Active Skill-Building Strengthen the Foundations of Resilience: Working Paper No. 13. ," National Scientific Council on the Developing Child, March 2015, www.developingchild.harvard.edu.

The next year, when we were back at school in-person, she struggled to make connections with peers. She tried to talk to students in her classes, but with masks covering our faces and most students already having friends from middle school, she felt stuck. She guessed everyone already had their friends and that there was no hope for community.

School became a dark and lonely place for her. It was one thing being alone at home, but it was worse feeling alone surrounded by other people.

A couple years later, as a junior in high school, she decided to go on an international class trip with students she didn't know. Away from the school environment, she was able to have deep conversations and form authentic connections with peers. She finally felt like she was finding her place in high school. Going on the trip was a risky leap of faith. But, it was the very thing she needed to find a sense of belonging and confidence.

## The Power of Words

My roommate and friend, Kat, gave me a book of poems by Mary Oliver last Christmas. She attached a note that said I have a natural gift for writing, and she hoped this book would inspire me to keep at it. People have told me they liked my writing before, but this felt different. This felt like she genuinely believed I could do something more than the occasional blog post. She saw something in me that I couldn't see in myself. Because of Kat's encouragement, I decided that the next year would be my Year of the Book—something I'd dreamed of my entire life.

Build Community

That is proof of a strong community. Community has the power to change the trajectory of someone's life. One simple encouragement, one sacred friendship, can change everything. You wouldn't be reading these words today if it wasn't for the kind words from a member of my community.

Our words have the power to kill and destroy, but also to bring life. We can all think of that person who has changed our lives with a sentence. My hope is that your mind drifts to the person who has encouraged you, checked in on you, and showed up for you. If someone doesn't come to mind, I hope you become brave and ask for help. Take a risk and send that email or text. Don't be distraught by the one "no" you receive. Keep fighting the good fight. Be that one person for someone else, and you will likely find that it comes back in a perfect circle.

Often, we walk into a party, a new small group, or an unfamiliar social situation and overthink how others perceive us. We spend all our time telling ourselves lies about how people are judging what we are wearing or what we are saying or that no one wants to include us in conversation. How much would change if we walked into a room thinking about how to better include others, compliment someone, or ask a question about someone's life? The surprising fix to finding supportive friends is *being* a supportive friend.

## Ask for Help

Help comes in many forms. Like I said before, we aren't meant to do this life alone. It may be difficult, especially at first, but sometimes, we must muster up the courage to ask

43

for help. Becoming vulnerable and committing to community is gut-wrenching and sometimes painful, but it is also deeply important and rewarding.

When I moved into my house in Seattle with five roommates, I bought an Ikea dresser. Those of you who like building Ikea furniture are simply wrong (sorry, not sorry). The endless directions with no words, the hundreds of screws and knobs—it is *stress-inducing*. I went the first month in my house without a dresser, and my room didn't have a closet. I literally lived out of my suitcases for a month because I couldn't figure out how to build the dresser on my own. I didn't know where to start, and I didn't know how to ask for help from these girls that had already given me above and beyond.

One day, after getting home from a long hike, two of them *offered* to build my dresser. No strings attached—they just wanted my room to feel homier and could see right through my stress and procrastination. They sat there on my bedroom floor and, piece after piece, spent four hours of their time building my dresser. I have never been more thankful in my life. Two people I didn't even know two months ago offered to help me with something I couldn't do myself.

Finally, I realized, this is the community I prayed for.

In college, I needed deeper help as I struggled to process my parents' divorce, so I found a local therapist. My counselor was extremely calm, gentle, and had the sweetest eyes, along with the most truthful words. She would often leave me with a challenge at the end of our time together, something to send me off into my week. This week, in particular, I talked about how agonizing it was to tell my friends about my parents' divorce. I never knew I would feel embarrassed about this, but it was as if shame enveloped me. I hated talking about it. I would walk by the lake and into the dining hall, imagining my friends and classmates seeing right through me. They could see every crack and loose screw in me, every emotion, hurt, and brokenness.

"Everyone knows I'm hurting," I thought to myself. "How could I possibly act normal when any sense of normalcy seems to be slipping right out from under me?"

My counselor challenged me to tell just one person weekly about my parents' divorce. This seemed manageable, I presumed. A few close friends already knew, but I needed to let in a few more people in my circle.

Being my dramatic self, I first texted my friend Charlotte about meeting to talk with me about something. Charlotte is the calmest, gentlest, and most patient soul you will ever meet. Sunshine in human form, quite frankly. Charlotte scurried to my little college dorm room down the hall and plopped on my twin bed. Tears filled my eyes as I told her what was going on. She listened with big eyes and simply held my hand. No words were spoken, but none needed to be. Her eyes, too, became teary, and that was all I ever needed. She was with me completely, and she felt what I felt. In that moment, I realized that asking for support from my community was nothing to be afraid of—in fact, it was exactly what was missing.

Day by day, week by week, and one by one, I let people in. I walked around the lake with them, cried, laughed, and hugged them. And one by one, I was healing.

Telling our stories heals us, bonds us, and allows us to feel joy when we can't feel it for ourselves.

In the book of Romans, a letter written by Paul geared toward a divided community of Jews and Gentiles, he writes, "Rejoice with those who rejoice, and mourn with those who mourn" (Romans 12:15 [NIV]).[5]

Isn't this what community is truly about? I challenge you to celebrate others, with all the themed drinks and parties your heart desires. And cry with others, too. My friends in college cried with me often—it was the mark of deep community. They brought laughter when I couldn't find it for myself.

Community is hard and intimate and vulnerable. Letting people in is one of the scariest things I've done. But every time I told my story and was looked back in the eyes, I found joy and peace. It's not simply about letting others in. It's also about *who* you let in. Choose, for your community, those that will lovingly look you in the eyes and assure you, "You are so strong. And you'll be okay, even though this isn't what you want." Choose those who will offer little hints of light in challenging conversations. When joy is hard to find yourself, it can be easier to find in community.

During my parents' divorce, I had the closest relationship with Jesus that I'd ever had because I let Him into every crack

---

5 Romans 12:15 (NIV)

and aching piece of my heart. We would meet together in the mornings over a Bible, journal, and coffee and sort through what was going on in my life. It works the same as with in-person people, only even better, because Jesus is the perfect friend. And while people on this earth fail us often, He never does. I found peace and security when I opened my broken heart and let Him sew it back together. Asking people for help and letting them in can lead to community, and asking Jesus for help and letting Him into your heart can lead to the greatest friendship of all time. I have never turned back, and am forever thankful.

## Wrap-Up

When you feel isolated, like no one cares about you, take *one* leap of faith. You might not find your best friends overnight, but you might feel a little bit more connected, a little bit closer to your thriving self within a community. Right where you live, groups exist to help you build community. Young Life is a national organization ready to help you live fully in community - there is probably a group near you. I hold onto the hope that groups at school, church, and sports are built to connect you to others, to pull you out of isolation. I have hope that there are adults in your life who want to listen and who care about you. Everyone needs a friend, and I hold onto the hope of a world where everyone has one.

There will be an opportunity at the end of this book to join my community. I hope that you choose to connect with me and those that are also looking for ways to live joyful lives amidst change.

I am so sorry if you've had a bad experience with friends, adults, or church. This world is full of broken relationships and broken people. I hope and pray that we can continue the search for community, even when people hurt us. It is hard, but it is deeply worth the search. Take a risk, let in the right people, be a friend to others, and live life always in search of community. Just like a seed needs certain conditions to thrive, community is one of the best choices you can make for yourself to create the best conditions for *you* to thrive. Life can indeed be beautiful when we get to experience it through more eyes than just ours.

## JOURNAL IT OUT:

- How could you take a risk and be a better friend to someone this week?
- Who is one person you could ask for help this week?
- Who is one person you could share something you're going through with?

# Chapter 6:
# Revel in the Little Moments

The little moments are really the big ones. The holding of hands on walks. The "this song made me think of you" texts. The spontaneous adventures to Party City to plan a St. Patrick's Day party. The moments we didn't plan. The moments we didn't schedule. The moments where we laugh really hard with no sense of "wasting time." I want to be a person who savors these precious minutes of my day, who revels in the joys of everyday life. They might seem small, but when we look back, they are massive.

I've always been a sucker for really over-dramatizing pretty much everything. A starry night? The most beautiful thing I've ever seen. A room full of friends having a tender moment together? A spiritual encounter. In the ninth-grade classroom I teach in, when a student chugs a gallon of milk? A heavenly moment where everything is okay, even for a second.

I used to think all people saw life this way, saw every moment as having a deep meaning and symbolism. Then I learned that most other people see these everyday things as, simply, the sky, or friends hanging out, or ninth graders being ninth graders. My highs are high, and my lows…well, they are low. And I wallow in pain when others would have moved on.

My emotions have gotten the best of me quite often. Growing up, I would feel so sorry for myself I would make myself sick. When I would get sent to my room, I would cry and cry. I think a part of me loved being the victim. I loved being sad, because it meant I could take time to feel deeply.

This continued into adolescence. When I was seventeen, my brother ate all the cheese pizza my mom left for us in the kitchen. I firmly believed he did this because he didn't care about me as a person and was blatantly disregarding my feelings and existence. In reality, he may have just been a fifteen-year-old boy, not thinking it was a big deal to eat all the pizza after a sweaty basketball practice. I took his actions as an insult, and stormed off in my Honda CRV, listening to my "Sad Taylor Swift Songs" playlist and crying at Chick-fil-A. I wonder what the drive-through workers thought.

I have definitely let my emotions negatively overtake me at times by falling in love too quickly, wallowing in sadness for days too long, and dismissing logic in decision-making. But I have also come to see that my emotions are one of my most beautiful parts.

I love that, from my eyes, every morning sunrise is God talking to me. Every laugh I hear at school between friends is a glimpse of heaven. Every sip of coffee is precious. That one line I read in a good book gives me butterflies and goosebumps. The a capella song around Christmas time in an echoey church makes me believe in redemption. This is heightened especially when shared in community. The candlelit funeral of a sorority sister urges me to bring people together with my words and prayers. Life's unforgiving circumstances lead to early mornings clinging to God's truth. My friends' loss and heartache bring tears to my eyes as I sit with them. I choose to feel these moments to their fullest, and my life is all the more vibrant for it.

## A Gas Station in Florida

In my senior year of college, my tight-knit group of eight girlfriends made the trek from South Carolina to Captiva, Florida, for Spring Break. This was the last spring break of college, so we were excited to spend quality time together. On the road trip, we listened to Taylor Swift and throwbacks, talked about life, and stopped at some questionable gas stations.

When we got to Florida, we stopped at a gas station because my friend Maggie and I had to use the restroom. There was toilet paper on the floor and a line of about eight people.

Faintly, I heard a whisper from one of the stalls. "Can anyone help?"

After the second call for help—everyone in front of me was staring idly at the wall—I said, "Yes?"

An older woman replied in despair, "I'm stuck."

I went into go-time mode and asked, "Okay, can you open the door?"

"I can't stand up."

With no other option, I got on my knees on that dirty bathroom floor and crawled under the stall. I helped her stand up, helped her pull her pants up, and unlocked the door for her to go wash her hands. She was abundantly thankful and told me I looked about the same age as her granddaughter. Her husband was waiting for her outside the door, so she was well cared for after that.

Maggie and I busted out of the bathroom and ran back to the car, dying laughing. In no way were we laughing at the lady—if anything, I felt terribly sorry for her. But Maggie had captured a photo of my legs hanging out from under the stall door, and we were cackling at the image. Did this really just happen? Did I really just army-crawl across a nasty bathroom floor? Yes, I did, and all my friends agreed: it was a very "Smith" thing to happen.

I could have let this moment pass me by. I could have sat silently with everyone else in line, waiting for someone else to help. I could have been disgusted by the dirty bathroom floors, frustrated that I was the only one who chose to deal with the situation. However, this moment at a gas station in Florida became one of our funniest college memories. We can miss God's moments for us if we don't choose to help, if we don't see the joy in difficult moments, if we don't stop to laugh every once in a while.

Author and speaker Hannah Brencher puts it this way in her Advent Devotional: "I am often guilty of assuming there are days on my calendar that hold no weight, just days that act as a barrier from the days I really, really want to live out. But this could not be further from the truth…All the things that are coming up this season have already been pre-planned out by God, and the best thing you and I can do to honor the planning is to pay close attention and lean in. We will miss the miracles if our heads stay stuck in our phones. God wants to show Himself to you in the mundane and the extraordinary. He wants to be in all of it."[6]

## Lighthearted Friends

I have certain friends constantly reminding me of the truth that every moment is a chance to experience something magical. One of these friends is a lifelong friend, Maggie—not to be confused with the Maggie from college in the story above. Maggie and I grew up next door to each other. Our childhood was filled with climbing trees, running between each other's houses to see who had the best snacks, and making up dances and performances for our parents, who were kind enough to applaud along.

One summer in Northern Michigan, where Maggie's family spent their summers, we were walking back from the beach, late at night, as teenagers. We were laughing so hard about something that we literally both peed our pants. There have not been many moments where I have laughed so hard in my entire life. I think I can count them on my hand. If I had to bet, they were probably all with Maggie.

As we've grown into adults, we have remained close and even went on a road trip from San Francisco to Denver a few years ago.

---

6  Hannah Brencher, "No Random Days." Daily Advent Devotional. December 1, 2022. https://www.hannahbrenchercreative.com/advent

We are different in so many ways, and she has always brought out an excitement for life in me. Maggie is the kind of friend that *lives*. I mean, really lives. She doesn't need a lot of prior plans. She doesn't talk the talk. She takes action. She's quick on her feet at all times—both literally, hiking up mountains, and metaphorically, with the perfect, sarcastic comeback. She pushes me to let go, to experience the present, and to not think so much. I am always in awe of how friendships can wind and change and shift, but yet root you in some way. During one of many hours on the road, we laughed and reminisced about how we have grown into ourselves but are still very much the same. Maggie is still confident and quirky. She will always be the improviser—opening a can of beans with a knife or driving our rental car through a self-invented gravel "road."

Maggie taught me to laugh, and re-teaches me that lesson often. When I begin to take life too seriously, she lovingly lets me be fully present in a moment and reminds me to breathe. When I was in my school work, dreading the next day's algebra exam, she would casually pull me outside to play Flashlight Tag.

"You don't have to take everything around you so seriously!" she has told me a hundred times.

Who we have around us shapes us. Not only is it essential to have people around us who are moving in the same direction in life, but we need people around us who are joy-bringers. We are constantly becoming the five people we spend the most time around. Who are those five people for you? Are they people who bring joy to your life or take away from it? Do you laugh a lot with the people you're around?

## Laugh like a Child

Maggie is not the only one who teaches me to laugh. I recently saw on Instagram an unquoted statistic that said, "Three-year-olds laugh forty times a day, and forty-year-olds laugh three times a day. Let us be more like children." I don't know if that is statistically accurate, but I don't doubt it. Jesus knew what he was doing when he said, "Let the children come to me" (Luke 18:16 [NLT]).[7] We have a lot to learn from those little balls of joy.

I teach four classes of eighth-grade Spanish this year. I was initially intimidated by teaching middle school, but while it has been challenging in many ways, I have loved the younger, more childlike energy they bring to my days. It is quite a drastic change from tenth-grade sleepiness and sluggishness. In my class the other day, I looked over, and a student was pulling his pants off in the middle of class. Yes, he had shorts underneath, but I took one look and started laughing my head off. All the kids started laughing too, and it became a moment we now bring up over and over.

Over my years of teaching middle and high school, countless hilarious moments have reminded me why I love what I do. In every one of those moments, I could have gotten overwhelmed. I could have stressed over not sticking to the agenda, that we were going to get behind, and that they would never learn

7  Luke 18:16 (NLT)

Spanish. And every time, after a random, spontaneous moment where we take a few moments to laugh and "be," I'm reminded that *that* is even more important. When we spontaneously decide to go get donuts in the middle of class, we are building community. That community is more vital than any lesson plans I had.

While I care about my students' learning, I care even more about their joy. I hope that they remember laughing with me, more than my impatience. I hope I'm a bright spot in their day or an adult they can trust. I hope that, more often than not, I let them be kids. They already have enough pressure and expectations put on them.

I often look back at the days at work where I laughed a lot as my favorite. Young people bring that out of me, and I'd much rather create a classroom of joy than rigor and stress. But far too often, I get upset that they didn't follow the rules, talked out of turn, or didn't prepare for class. While holding them accountable is necessary, why do I let these little mishaps steal my joy? Why do I redirect them from being kids and sharing a moment of laughter to instead work and "stay on track?"

This can be applied to all parts of our lives. How often do we let our agendas and plans disconnect us from life's spontaneous moments? When was the last time you laughed really hard, for longer than expected, and didn't cut yourself short?

In a sermon I heard recently, the pastor shared that happiness is an emotion based on circumstances, but joy is gratitude rooted in grace, no matter our circumstance. Let's not get so stuck in our plans that we don't allow ourselves true joy. Forcing happiness is not true joy. Joy comes from gratitude despite the circumstance you are in. This is where the little spontaneous moments come in. Try being thankful for those little sparks of joy, the moments where you forget everything going on and laugh at an eighth grader taking his pants off—that is more profound joy. Take that, thank God, and find deeper satisfaction than trying to be "happy," than trying to be "on track." For a sweet, simple moment, all is well with the world. When life is closing in on you, you need to still allow yourself to laugh really hard at something.

How easily could I have let that moment pass by telling the kids to get back on track, to follow the plan? Where are our priorities? What margin do we leave in our lives for joy to creep in?

Taking hold of your life often means leaving space—committing to letting your plans change to allow the light to seep in the cracks. When our lives are so structured, there is no margin for joy. I promise, no matter what, there are little hints of light right where you are—if you allow them to exist, they will brighten your world.

## My Love Story

When I first met my fiancé Brian, I noticed how much joy he brought to every room he was in. When people first asked me how our relationship was going, I would say, "We always have so much fun together and laugh a lot." While there are many important things in a relationship, I am guilty of taking things far too seriously and getting too deep about everything. After spending time with Brian, my mouth hurt from smiling so much, and the lightheartedness of our connection brought so much peace.

One of my earliest memories of our relationship was laughing together while cooking dinner, a simple evening. We were cooking dinner, dancing, hugging, and laughing. Then Brian looked at me with the most sincere smile.

"I love how much fun we can have, just cooking dinner," he said.

From the very beginning, Brian taught me the importance of not taking life too seriously—to enjoy every mundane moment. It's so important to surround ourselves with people that bring out new sides of our personalities.

Brian is the type of person who wakes up in the morning ready to conquer the day. One of my favorite quirks of his is how he excitedly jumps up and down in the morning, naming everything we get to do that day.

"We get to work out! We get to make coffee! We get to eat breakfast! We get to watch football!" He finds joy in life's simple things and can laugh me out of my negative mood swings.

He's not positive in an annoying way. He doesn't tell me to get over it when I am down. Rather, he is joyfully steady, always there. When I'm feeling off, cranky, or sad for no particular reason, he is patiently *there*, steadying my rise and fall. Early in our relationship, we realized that he overcame conflict and arguments much faster than I did. While I am a dweller, he quickly forgives and moves on.

Now, he will hold my hand and ask me, "Is there anything else you want to say? Anything else we need to talk about? Are you ready to move on, or do you want to sit here a little bit longer?"

Brian is logical, curious, loyal, and consistent. I am emotional, indecisive, and loving. We are both independent, caring, and thoughtful in our unique ways. He is a "pros and cons" list, and I am a gut decision. He dwells on the positive, and I sit in the pain. His feelings are stable, and mine look more like a heart rate monitor. He fills in where I do not excel and reminds me of Christ's forgiveness often. His actions not only follow his words but often come before them. He's the steadiest person I know. I don't know what I did to deserve his love, but I thank God every single day for him.

Our love story is not all rainbows and butterflies, however. We have worked really hard to love each other well. We have been in conflict with each other and ended up stronger for it. We have asked the hard questions, forgiven, and enjoyed each other's differences. We've met and loved each other's friends, flown across the country multiple times, traveled to different countries, hiked tall mountains, and skied down them, too. We've handled family dynamics, taken care of each other when we're sick, and seen each other at our lowest of lows. And yes, we've celebrated each others' successes, surprised each other with coffee, and written love notes every month (Brian's only missed a few). I can't wait to keep learning about each other. We are the best team I know.

## Wrap-Up

Finding the people who complement us and force us to laugh when we don't want to is hard. It's important to know ourselves and which side we lean toward—spontaneous laughter or deep emotions. I, for one, lean toward deep feelings, and that brings many gifts to me and others in my life. My ability to feel every part of an experience and see beauty and depth in the simple is incredible. It's one of my favorite parts of myself. However, to complement this aspect of my personality, I must find people who bring out the opposite: simple, lighthearted joy that still has deep meaning. If you are someone who flees emotion at all costs, you may need to find someone who teaches you to sit in your feelings.

My students, Brian, Maggie, and so many others have taught me that leaving margins for spontaneity is what true joy is made of. Joy does not mean that everything is perfect. Some of my deepest joy has been felt simultaneously with my deepest pain. At the end of my days, I hope I laughed more than I wallowed. I hope I let myself and others slow down despite an agenda. I hope I left margins in my schedule for spontaneous joy. I hope I look back at the little moments and see the beauty and truth: that they are really the big moments.

Feel the joy, the sadness, the heartbreak. Don't be afraid to let little moments become big ones. Stare in awe at the sunset. Revel in the presence of people you love. Don't be scared to over-dramatize your life. Don't let emotion overtake you, but let it drive you to live a whole and meaningful life. Find joy in every part of your journey.

## *JOURNAL IT OUT:*

- Write about the last time you laughed really hard. What happened?
- What is a little thing you're thankful for right now?
- Are you someone who sits in your emotions, or do you like to keep things more lighthearted? What could you do to embrace the side you don't lean toward?

# Chapter 7:
# Embrace Routine

You're probably thinking at this point, "Wow, you are really good at finding joy in all the small moments." But I'm writing this after coming out of a class full of eighth graders who wouldn't stop talking and kicking each other constantly. It was exhausting and infuriating, and I lost my patience, snapping at them—which, in turn, made me feel guilty.

We've all had those moments where we act in ways we don't approve of. In those moments, we don't even recognize ourselves. As a person writing a book on joy and a person who is seeking to find joy in life's changes, I don't *feel* a lot of joy right now.

What do you do when you don't feel joy? The first thing that came to my mind was that every single day is a new opportunity to find joy. Some days, joy does not come easily. Today is one of those days where I honestly don't feel a lot of joy. I feel defeated. I want to go home and sleep and numb the pain. But now, I can choose joy. I can choose hope. I can choose to take care of myself this afternoon. Tomorrow is a new day to find joy again.

Not only can we choose joy, but we can simply receive it. Joy is a gift, a fruit of the spirit from God. We don't have to work for it—we can rest and receive. Finding joy is a process, and there's no destination. I'm thinking about the verse "[His mercies] are new every morning" (Lamentations 3:23 [CSB]).[8] I'm thinking about the cycle of how God designed the days. I'm grateful for the way that the morning comes again, every single twenty-four hours. The consistency and stability of that are carrying me right now, and God designed it that way on purpose. I'm grateful that I have a morning and a fresh start to find joy tomorrow.

I see routines and rhythms as vehicles for finding joy every single day. I know routine might come with a boring connotation. In the last chapter, I even told you to leave room to be spontaneous, laugh, and revel in the small moments. However contradictory it may seem, these routines actually *can* be things that bring us joy in the long run. Things like going out to get coffee once a week because it makes you smile, playing tennis twice a week because you notice the mood boost it gives you after, or starting your day off journaling and reading the Bible, clinging to the truth that you feel lighter and at peace afterward can all be ways that routine can bring joy.

Beyond routines bringing us joy in and of themselves, keep in mind that without routine, we can't allow ourselves time to be spontaneous later. Routine and structure are what hold space for spontaneity. If we make a habit of leaving margins within our days, we have more time to help a friend in crisis, stop for a sidewalk conversation, or stay at lunch longer.

---

8  Lamentations 3:23 (CSB)

Imagine your perfect morning. I guarantee it's not rushing into work late and chugging coffee in traffic. It probably looks more like having time for yourself, making your favorite beverage, and sipping it in your favorite chair, feeling peace and calm. Routines can bring us constant joy, no matter where we are.

## 3 Contradictory Rules for Routines

At this point, you've probably realized that much of my advice contradicts my other advice. I am entirely aware of that and actually okay with it. That's how life goes—in some moments, one answer is right, and in others, it isn't. I never want to claim to be "right" about anything because every situation and person is unique. We are in constant flux and constantly have new and different needs. These "rules" for routine are really fake rules. Not because I don't believe in them but because they contradict themselves. On purpose.

That said, let's jump into some general rules when it comes to making effective routines:

1. Routines can't always depend on location, but it's nice when they can.

I love being on the go and having adventures, but I also crave routine and structure. In Education, we talk a lot about how implementing systems and routines in our classrooms is vital for students' success. It eases them into our classroom and gets them ready to learn. I've found that adults operate the same way—we just have a harder time being told what to do. As I've gotten older, I've valued being home, sleeping in my bed, and following my routine more and more.

However, this past summer I chose to travel for several weeks despite knowing that I would struggle being out of my routine. Instead of fretting that I wasn't home, I accepted that I was going to be on the go and clung to this verse from the gospel of John: "The Word became flesh and made His dwelling among us" (John 1:14 [NIV]).[9] The Message translation reads, "He moved into our neighborhood" (John 1:14 [MSG]).[10] This verse comforted me by reminding me that God was with me no matter where I was—Connecticut, Switzerland, or Canada. Because of Jesus, I could experience a relationship with God, which brings me the most peace and joy, no matter where I am or how my routine is changed.

Don't get me wrong—there were moments when it was hard to feel God's presence, especially when I couldn't spend as much time with Him. But, every day, I reminded myself that God dwells among us, that He is even with me in the airport, when I'm lonely and distracted. He never leaves us.

So, we can find peace without routines in a particular location. But routines are often special because of a place you go back to again and again. On my college campus, there was an authentic Japanese temple called "The Place of Peace" right up the sidewalk from my dorm room. The Place of Peace was built in 1984 and is the first Japanese temple ever to be dismantled and reconstructed in America. Like what?!

---

9   John 1:14 (NIV)
10   John 1:14 (MSG)

When I was in college, I made it part of my daily routine to visit the Place of Peace. In the early morning hours, I would scurry over to the wrap-around porch and bask in the quiet. I'm a sucker for mornings—the softness of the light sparkling off the green trees, the stillness before a college campus awakes with hustle, laughter, and to-dos. This place was a true place of peace for me throughout my sophomore year. I would find myself there often, around the same hour of the day, in every season of the year. Praying, meditating, watching the sunrise, and easing into my day in solitude.

I have a photo from fall, winter, spring, and summer sitting at the exact same location. Orange, yellow, and red leaves changed to white snow, to pink blooms, to luscious green in the blink of an eye. But my mornings, my deep breaths, and my time with my Creator stabilized me, even when my family stability was falling beneath me. I would often pray the same phrase on repeat: "Spirit, lead me where you want me to go today." This routine place became a reliable comfort amid my changing life. Sometimes, a particular place and a particular routine grounds us.

I'm sure every one of us has our own place of peace, that familiar place we go to—either in real life or in our minds—where we feel the calmest, least worried, and closest to God, the source of peace itself. For some of us, it's a serene place in nature. For others, it's the comfy living room chair where you pray. For me, it was a Japanese temple around the corner from my dorm room that carried me through the most challenging season of my life.

When we're on the journey for joy in day-to-day life, it might seem counterintuitive to seek routine. We think we need to do something spontaneous, out of the ordinary—climb Mt. Kilimanjaro or quit our jobs. And that's absolutely true sometimes. However, I've found that peaceful routines can bring us the most joy in our day to day. Find your little hints of light in your sacred places and grab onto them for dear life. Find the stability you can in a world that constantly changes.

2. Routines can't always depend on consistent timing, but it's nice when they can.

I am a morning person, through and through—so much so that I look forward to my coffee the following day when I go to bed. I love getting eight hours of sleep, which is why I go to bed so early. I revel in fully enjoying life before the world wakes up. The birds chirping, the sun rising, and the stillness of the sky makes my heart flutter with anticipation. I have my most intimate conversations with God in the morning, before our days have left us wrangled and distraught. For a moment, life has not begun to drag me down and I can talk to Him with a fresh slate, a clear conscience, and a purity of day that resembles evermore closely heaven above.

While I understand that you night owls may be shaking your heads at me, I firmly believe that how we start our days matters. What we feed our minds matters, especially in the mornings. There is a clear difference in my day when I start it by journaling, listening to worship music, and spending time with God, versus when I stare at Instagram, consuming a highlight reel of life that isn't reality.

Research from Harvard professor Gerald Zaltman shows 4–6 percent of our decisions are made consciously, and the other 94–96 percent are made subconsciously. Subconscious decisions influence your behavior, even though you don't realize it. This subconscious is running our lives, and it's made up of what we put in—images, movies, music, TV, etc. When I watch *Bachelor in Paradise* and take in all the relationship drama, I *subconsciously* find myself more anxious that my boyfriend will leave me for no reason. I find I am more likely to create drama in my life, even if it leads to nothing. Don't get me wrong, I love some good reality TV at times, but being aware of how *much* of it we are feeding ourselves is so important. When I focus more of my energy on reading my Bible and God's truth of forgiveness and mercy, I become a more gentle friend, loving girlfriend, and patient individual. It matters. And it changes us.

I believe that what we put in our minds in the morning, especially, has an even greater impact because it sets the tone for the rest of the day.

Imagine, for a moment, what your life would look like if it had a bit more peace. Peace is not the absence of busyness, but rest in the midst of chaos. It's our soul singing praises when our circumstances are not. No matter what change I'm going through, peace is abundant when I start my day with God.

Find what works for you. Maybe this means not checking your phone for the first twenty minutes of your day, creating time to sit down and eat breakfast, or making your bed every day. Watch what happens with your day. I hope you find that the more space you allow in the morning, the more resilience you will have to conquer anything life throws at you during the day.

While a morning routine grounds me, there are times in life when sticking to that routine is more challenging—like right now, as I'm writing this chapter. My house is currently infested with rats, and I'm not going to lie, these past couple weeks have felt overwhelming. I haven't been able to stay in my own home, and solutions—and exterminators—have been extremely tough to track down. We don't realize how much we rely on having a safe home until we don't have it anymore. Maintaining any type of routine has felt challenging.

My mornings might look different as I'm commuting from different houses and couch surfing, but I still try to stick to my routine as well as I can. One day last week, I got up early and went to Starbucks to read my Bible. Having this time in the morning refreshed my soul in a way I can't explain. Even if I don't have my own room and my own coffeemaker, I can still listen to podcasts in the morning and work out after the school day adjourns. While we can't control circumstances, we can try and maintain a routine, even if it feels different.

Maybe it's not even that we need *routine*. Maybe what we need is God. When life is good and dandy and no problems arise, routine is pretty easy to fall into. We naturally wake up, drink our coffee, and build our rhythms. The repetitive days of habit-building when life is going well become our anchor when life isn't going so well. When I get rats in my house, I lean on my habit of reading my Bible in the morning exponentially more than when I have my warm, cozy house to wake up to. When life gets hard, when it feels like the floors are slipping beneath me, I cling to my Bible like I need it to breathe. I crave moments alone with God when life is going astray. Maybe that's why James says in his book at the end of the Bible to rejoice when trials come (James 1:2).[11] Trials are what draw us closer to our Father. They are where we recognize that we can't do it alone. When all I have is a whisper deep inside of me saying, "God, I need you. I can't do this without Your strength," I find peace.

That's where those years of morning routines come most in handy: when doing them feels most inconvenient. I go to God in the mornings, and He is there, listening to every doubt, complaint and gasp for strength. "God, I can't do this alone," I tell Him, and in return, He sends me peace.

3. Routines can't be dependent on other people.

When I was living in Chile as an eighteen-year-old, I came face to face with a culture that views productivity and time differently from mine. One Saturday morning, my host mom, Ximena, told me that we were going to their friend Jenny's house for lunch later that day. Excitedly, I washed my face, put on clothes, and waited downstairs around 9 A.M. I soon realized that no one else had even begun to get ready. My host sister floated in and out of the kitchen in pajamas, my host dad went to run errands, and my host mom started cooking in the kitchen. I was confused. Hadn't we made a plan? Weren't we supposed to leave an hour ago?

---

11  James 1:2

We eventually got in the car around 12:30 P.M., and drove right past Jenny's house. My Spanish was subpar at the time, and I was still warming up to my new host family. I did muster up enough words to ask my host sister, "What are we doing?" She just shrugged her shoulders, but gave me a look like, "Smith, why does it matter?" And this was all I needed. We ended up at the beach, got out of the car, and started strolling on the sidewalk, waves crashing in front of us. We stopped to buy some ice cream, take pictures in the sand, and people watch.

I slowly began to realize that time did not control them. Plans were meant to be changed

On August 26, 2015, I wrote, "Coming from a monochronic society like the US, it is ingrained in me to need a schedule, need the details, the plans for the day, and to be on time. Time is singular; there isn't much wiggle room for change or delays. You leave when you say you're going to leave. You go eat lunch when you say you're going to eat lunch. You want to fill your day with 'things.' In Chile, a polychronic society, time has multiple layers. In fact, time does not control the people here, but they more or less control time. It's not so much about productivity but just living. It's not so much about getting to lunch by one o'clock. But stop at the beach for an hour before and get there when you get there. If you're having a really good conversation with someone, you don't leave even if you have somewhere to be. Whatever it is can wait. Time is not constricting."

The Chileans taught me well the spirit of leaving margins for spontaneity. Routines can ground me, but they can only depend on me, not other people. Throughout my time there, I had moments when I was upset that friends would be late, cancel on me, or our plans wouldn't get started until two hours later than we planned. My timing would get thrown off, and the plans I made didn't happen. Building a routine or expectations off of other people wouldn't work for me, there. But it was still up to me to get up and go on a run at some point that day, or spend time journaling in the morning whether my coffee was made quickly or not. Even if my day didn't look the same as I expected, I could still take hold of what I knew brought me peace. So, no matter what happened, I kept my routine and had my solid grounding.

Carve out space for your routines no matter what. If you get delayed and miss your scheduled gym time, go to the gym an hour later. Don't let your whole life be tied to a specific schedule that causes your mood to suffer when one thing gets thrown off.

Some days, we need to protect our time and say no. Some days, we need to loosen our reins on routine and say yes to something else. Don't let other people steal your peace, but don't let selfishness run your life. Find the joy in your routines when they become binding, and you will find abundant peace.

4.  Accept the days when routine doesn't happen.

Some days just don't go as planned. We've all been there. There's a day that comes that knocks you right off your feet. You wake up in the morning cranky and tired from a late night picking up a friend from the airport. You sleep past your alarm and don't have any time in the morning to be still. You sprint to your car, spill your coffee, and hit ten more minutes of traffic than usual. Everything that could go wrong in your job does, and you feel anger building inside you. You feel like you're bringing everyone down, but you really don't know how to stop.

In life, it is hard to give yourself grace. While we are all seeking and searching for a better way to live, we will always fall short of perfection. That's okay. So many of our days are like this, and while I hope and pray for better days in the future, I don't think reaching for perfection ever helps us.

There are constants in your life, no matter what, that can ground you, even on days when your routine doesn't happen. This next year, I am going to start what I'm calling an "aware" journal. This is just a fancy word for writing one time a day about the moments when I saw God. On days when nothing goes well, I am going to force myself to find one moment where I felt God with me, encouraging me and holding my hand. Clinging to joy means finding something that our eyes can't always see. This can be a constant routine, no matter what my day looks like.

Most days, I have time in the car. I try to be intentional about what I do in the car, either listening to a podcast or worship music.

There are certain phrases I repeat to myself throughout any day. Some are from scripture, some I've created, some are prayers I've clung to time and time again. One is, "I am a child of God (Psalm 82:6), loved by God (1 John 4:10), complete in Christ" (Colossians 2:10). Another one is "I can do hard things." Another one is, "Lord, give me patience right now." What we are telling ourselves matters, and it changes us.

More often than not, I have forced these phrases to replace more negative ones. *I don't want to do this. I can't do this.*

In his book *Soundtracks: the Surprising Solution to Overthinking,* New York Times Bestselling Author Jon Acuff tells us "those are called broken soundtracks, negative stories you tell yourself about yourself and your world. They play automatically without any invitation or effort from you. Fear does not take work. Doubt does not take work. Insecurity does not take work."[12]

He goes on to offer advice on how to interrupt negative thinking:

"Retire your broken soundtracks. Replace them with new ones. Repeat them until they're as automatic as the old ones. Retire. Replace. Repeat."[13]

Last night, I woke up at three o'clock in the morning and couldn't fall back asleep. Lies and anxiety were attacking me from all sides. I didn't know what to do, so I let them flood me like a river: *You aren't safe. Your situation will never be fixed. You are not loved. You are a terrible person.* And, then, a well deep within me whispered truth: *You are safe. You are protected. You are loved.* I repeated that fifty times, until I fell asleep. These

---

12  Jonathan Acuff, Soundtracks: The Surprising Solution to Overthinking (Grand Rapids, MI: Baker Books, a division of Baker Publishing Group, 2021), 22

13  Jonathan Acuff, Soundtracks: The Surprising Solution to Overthinking (Grand Rapids, MI: Baker Books, a division of Baker Publishing Group, 2021), 25.

truths, statements I repeat to myself, are constants no matter what. They are routines, in a sense.

## Wrap-Up

Routines can help ground you whether it's a certain space, time, or phrases. Consistent spaces can bring comfort, and the way we start our days shapes our thoughts.

In order to find the best routine, find what's best for *you*.

Choose your consistent space: whether a living room chair or a place in nature.

Choose your timing: ideally right when you wake up, even if it's five minutes of silence.

Choose yourself: start small and don't let your routines depend on other people

Choose to accept that much of our lives is out of our control.

When routines that require time and space don't work, when life gets in the way, we can trust ourselves to be constant. Our minds and our hearts live with us no matter where we are. When we can't control life's circumstances, we can control how we speak to ourselves. Let our inner voices be ones of hope, strength, and love.

Once our outer worlds have more consistency and our inner worlds find rhythm, we can have the margin in life to learn more about ourselves. This will lead to the greatest adventure of all - falling in love with ourselves.

## JOURNAL IT OUT:

- What does your ideal morning look like?
- Write about a place that is special to you. Why and what memories do you have there?
- What is a phrase you want to repeat to yourself throughout the day? Put it somewhere you can see it—mirror, phone screen, etc.

# Chapter 8:
# Fall in Love with Yourself

I lived in Washington, D.C. the summer after my junior year of college. I went through a breakup in the last couple weeks of school, immediately went on a twelve-day road trip with my childhood best friend from San Francisco to Denver, then the *next* day jumped on a plane to intern in D.C. for the summer. This was "classic Smith" and shocked absolutely no one. I think the person it shocks the most is 25-year-old Smith writing this today.

That summer in D.C., I was on fire for life. I had just gone through a breakup, so I felt like I was entering into a new era of "Smith." For the first time in a long time, I felt like I would go wherever Jesus was leading me. My life was wholly His, with no distractions, full steam ahead. My internship didn't run on Wednesdays, so naturally, I decided to take a bus an hour south and volunteer at the D.C. Dream center with at-risk kids. Now, in my old age of twenty-five with a full-time job, I would plop myself right on the couch on any day off. But that summer, I was fearless and ready to make an impact. The D.C. Dream Center is a community center in one of the roughest neighborhoods in D.C. It's over the Anacostia River, and no metro line runs to the neighborhood. They are physically cut off from the rest of society, isolating residents physically and socially. According to the D.C. Dream Center website, their mission is to "inspire youth and adults to dare to dream, equipping them to reach their God-given potential."

I volunteered at the Wednesday Reconciliation Luncheon, where I helped prepare and serve food for an interfaith and intercultural meal. Anyone and everyone was invited to this luncheon. Pastors and laypeople from all over the city gathered together for a meal and intentional conversation. Everyone at the lunch was unique in skin color, thought, religious practice, and denomination, yet they gathered to eat together. It was beautiful to witness how these different people ended up finding that they had so much in common—family, faith, even love of mashed potatoes. Blinders and masks fall off when people gather around a table and talk. When our sole purpose is gathering to love, instead of gathering to argue that we're right, the world looks a little bit more like heaven.

At the luncheon, I met another girl serving food who was a few years younger than me. She was asking questions about college and life as an adult, and I learned that she lived with her dad in D.C. for the summer. Her dad was attending the luncheon and used to be a pastor in D.C. After the luncheon, she introduced me to her father. We chatted for a while, and I immediately felt calm in their presence. They asked how I was getting home, and I told them I would take the bus. Agreeing to come with me on the bus, they invited me to a worship night at their church, held in the basement of a local coffee shop. The service was mainly geared toward the unhoused in D.C.; she and her father told me stories of the people they've come to know and love there on Wednesday nights.

Without hesitating, I agreed to go with these strangers to a basement worship night (do as I say, not as I do, kids). We had a couple hours to spare before, so we grabbed a coffee in the stunning Union Station. We talked about internships and divorce, and trusting God with our lives.

While walking over to the coffee shop, I didn't know what to expect—but when I got there, I entered a room full of some of the most wonderful people I have ever met. I listened to their stories as we ate a warm meal in the dim twinkly lights of the basement. And then, all together, we sang our hearts out to worship songs. No matter where we are in life, our faith unites us. Tears welled in my eyes as I looked around at my new friends and at the father-daughter duo that invited me.

Trusting God is scary, especially amidst change. But it led me there, and I'm thankful.

Taking the time to fall in love with life and with myself again after a breakup led me to a day of adventure I never could have planned. I could've sat inside every day that summer, wishing I was in a relationship, but I chose not to dwell on what was or what would be. Joy finds us when we choose to live our lives *now*. Not only does joy find us, but it lives within us and leads our lives.

If my friends I met that day ever read this, thank you for showing me the power of falling back in love with myself. I chose not to let singleness rob me of joy. Instead, I got out there—exploring coffee shops, volunteering with kids at the Dream Center, diving into my internship, enjoying happy hours with old and new friends, and spending weekends exploring DC. All these things, subtle in nature, made me more confident. I was my own best companion, and I grew to learn that I'd always be okay so long as I enjoyed being with myself.

Life with God is never dull, rarely easy, and the greatest adventure I've been on.

In my senior year of college, when I was fretting about the unknown, I remember a distinct conversation with my counselor. Remembering my time in D.C., I told her that I knew I would be okay no matter where I was because I genuinely enjoyed being with myself. This doesn't mean I don't get lonely or anxious, but I never let being alone stop me from doing what I want to do.

## Learn about Yourself

When I first moved to Seattle, there seemed like endless possibilities for exploration. People were shocked that I had already seen more of Washington state than lifelong natives. Even during the COVID-19 pandemic and flexible work hours, I would take myself skiing three or four times a week. Those peaceful moments on the mountain by myself were serene. I would watch the sunset at a park I've never been to. I would walk to bakeries and try their specialty croissants. I went to churches and small groups by myself to meet a few more people. There is nothing greater than community and experiencing life with other people, but true joy is not being reliant on having people to do things with all the time. We are with ourselves more than anyone else in this lifetime. If you like being with anyone, I hope it's you.

After years of being around other women my age and younger, I found that I might be in the minority in liking myself. Not that I'm perfect at it; I have my fair share of negative thoughts about myself. But confidence and self-worth are struggles I see over and over with young women, especially with teen girls. In middle school, girls would always need friends to go to the bathroom with them, get changed for sports, or do just about anything. You know what they always say: girls travel in packs.

I never understood this. I preferred to go by myself. So, what was so different about me, and how did I become this way?

My grandma gave me a journal on Easter Sunday in first grade. It had a little lock and a giant Easter egg on the front. I went home that night and wrote down *everything*—the drama going on at school, how I felt when I got sent to my room for being too tired, the devastation of Georgia losing to Auburn, and my little brother being annoying on his fifth birthday. My parents often found me huddled up in my room with a flashlight and a pen, journaling under my covers. It was my solace, my place of reflection, my own little inner world coming out on the pages.

When it really comes down to it, I've always been on a quest to learn more about myself, who I am, and how I operate in the world. Self-reflection came naturally to me, even as a seven-year-old, and it gave me intrinsic self-worth that didn't come from other people. I have always craved to deeply know myself, often reflecting on my life, behaviors, and inner peace.

Maybe you lean in the opposite direction. Maybe it is painful, even frightening, to imagine reflecting on who you are. Maybe you'd prefer to focus on the fun of life, surround yourself with people at all times, and focus on living instead of looking backward. There is no shame in that tendency, but I think there is someone deep inside each of us who is waiting for us to get to know them, to fall in love with them. We have to get through all the messiness to find the beauty that is our true selves. You were created intimately and uniquely, and there is something magical about who you are—you just need to find it. I guarantee that when you do, you will fall in love with who you are.

When life is changing and seasons come and go, you are also evolving as a person. There might be negative feelings about who we are becoming, but I urge you to lovingly and curiously take the time to learn about who you are right now. Just like how our friends change over time and how we are constantly learning and enjoying new versions of them, we must also be on the quest to discover who we are in each new season of our life. How have you changed? How have you grown? How have hard things made you into a better version of yourself? This is where the real magic happens—when we let change lead to joy, and we let joy change who we are.

## New Definition for Bravery

Sometimes, learning about yourself feels like talking to a stranger. I used to be so brave. In high school, I never wanted to get married because I felt so complete in myself. At 18, I moved to Chile by myself for a year. During my first year of college, I introduced myself to anyone I hadn't met. That summer in D.C., I went to Philadelphia alone for a weekend—I spent two nights in a hotel, went sightseeing, and ate meals in restaurants alone. I took a Greyhound bus back to D.C. and met who I thought was the love of my life.

While I know I could tap into my brave self if needed, as I write this now, tucked away in my room, I feel less brave than I used to be.

Since my wilder youth, I have felt a desire to settle down that I've never felt before. I desire a deep and rich community, a few good friends, a job I could stay in for at least a few years, and a serious relationship moving toward marriage. My tolerance for socializing has noticeably gone down, and to be honest, I don't quite know what to do about the changes in myself. Did I turn old and boring overnight? Did my life peak a few years ago, and is it already going downhill at age twenty-five? Did I somehow become less brave?

Or maybe…do I just have the wrong idea of bravery?

Maybe bravery is not just jumping into a new experience, but also being okay in the silence. Spending mornings the same way every day—coffee to Bible to rushing into my car with wet hair. Devoting my life to making teenagers feel seen, valued, and known. Walking around my neighborhood in the Seattle green dew. Falling in love as the leaves change colors. Exposing the messy parts of myself to a few close friends. Missing and calling friends and family. Doing chores on Sundays and going to Trader Joe's to buy more chocolate ice cream. Eating Thai food and watching *The Bachelorette* by myself on a Friday night. Learning how to budget. Following Jesus.

## Wrap-Up

Maybe being brave isn't what I thought it always was. Maybe I don't need to portray an adventurous life on social media. Maybe I can learn to be content and lean into this nudge to ground myself. Maybe, just maybe, being brave is learning and falling in love with who I am. Maybe it's finding joy in my regular, everyday life.

Just because my definition of brave has changed over the years doesn't mean I'm less brave. It means I'm a new version of brave. And I'm learning to love this new version of Smith, too.

## *JOURNAL IT OUT:*

- What are three adjectives you would use to describe yourself right now?
- What is something new you've learned about yourself recently?
- When was the last time you did something brave? (Remember, there are multiple definitions of brave)

# Chapter 9:
# Fight the People Pleaser
# Tendency

When I was in sixth grade, a classmate bit me in the arm at the lunch table. It caught me off guard, kind of hurt, and shocked me more than anything. She was just trying to be silly, but my little eyes started welling with tears.

I tried not to make a big scene, but felt a full-on cry coming on. I hurried out to the playfield for recess. I couldn't hold it in anymore, and before I knew it, a teacher saw me crying, and I told her what had happened. I got escorted to the clinic and was picked up from school there.

When I got home, my mom wanted the full story. I was way more concerned about what my classmate would say the next day than my bite mark. Would she be mad that I told the teacher on her? Would she feel embarrassed and spread rumors about me? Would she never be my friend again?

We talked on our home phones that evening. My classmate began to profusely apologize for biting me, but I stopped her. "No, no, it's okay! I want to apologize to *you*. I just don't want you to be mad at me for telling on you. I hope we can still be friends." She agreed that, of course, we could still be friends. Everything at school was the exact same the next day, as if nothing had happened between us.

As silly as this story is, it proves a point. I was more worried about a fractured relationship than taking care of myself.

I like to think I've grown up since then, but I probably haven't much. Far too often, I don't say what I mean to save face or to save a friendship, but this isn't just because I'm a nice person. A deeper, icky part to this isn't so pretty: I tell people what they want to hear because I want to be *liked,* and I don't want to deal with conflict. I am a self-diagnosed people-pleaser, constantly tip-toeing around so as not to ruffle any feathers. When I look deep within myself, I'd much rather have other people like me than do what's right for myself.

During my freshman year of college, I got thrown into a whirlwind of meeting hundreds of people over the first few months. There are endless possibilities, places, and people to be with. Option overload hit hard. When I was with my boyfriend, I missed out with my friends. When I was with friends, I was missing out on what other friends were doing. No relationship ever felt "enough" for me, and I was always left unsatisfied in the present moment.

When I moved to Seattle and began to date again, I was determined to enter into my next relationship fully present, unlike how distractedly I approached my college boyfriend. I wanted to allow myself to *enjoy* just being with my partner. I knew that if

I didn't rein in my people-pleasing tendencies, they would ruin my relationship again. I tended to get so hung up on making *everyone* happy that I ended up not letting myself be happy, and I had to break that habit.

Kicking a people-pleasing habit meant, first and foremost, that I had to be in a relationship with someone who was truly my best friend *and* fit into my community. Even if those two things are true, the next step was *allowing* myself to miss out on things with friends and being okay with it.

I so deeply desired to be in a relationship, but to really have that, I had to be okay with the fact that when we start dating someone, we simply have less time for everything we did in our single life. Does this mean we drop off the face of the earth right when we start dating someone? Not at all, and I wouldn't recommend that. It just means we might have to refine and adjust our priorities. For me, this looked like focusing on my closest friendships. I had less time to meet new people or attend big parties, but way more time to sit with my three best friends and say, "Let's *really* talk," and dive deep into what's *really* going on.

Although I was smitten, it took me several months to settle into my relationship with Brian. At month two, I called one of my best friends, who asked me how it was going with him. I said I was so happy—life felt new, exciting, and different. But I was still navigating how to balance having a new boyfriend, maintaining current friendships, and handling all other routine parts of life. Despite my conscious attempts to find balance, I felt overwhelmed and still often felt the need to please everyone. I felt like I was constantly disappointing my friends by saying no. My friend replied, "Right now, the relationship is new, but one day, he will just be another special person in your life."

This struck a chord. Change has a way of calming down and becoming normal, like a ripple of water that settles after the stone is thrown. We are adaptable, ready to adjust, and able to invite a "new normal" in. It might take time, and that's okay. Let's be gentle as we ease into change—even if it's a good change, like becoming less of a people-pleaser.

## You're Allowed to Prioritize Yourself

Four months into our relationship, Brian and I were supposed to go to Whistler, Canada, for a ski weekend with friends. But after Brian tested positive for COVID-19, we drove back to Seattle the very same day. I knew I truly loved him when I was still excited to be with him for the next three days in isolation, watching movies. I love our ski trips and adventures, but I love him even more.

Instead of hitting the slopes, we stayed in all weekend. I should tell people more often that I'm going on trips and then stay in with my favorite person, stocking up on Gatorade and mac n' cheese, making TikToks and playing 50 questions. Or better yet, I should just have weekends like that and not apologize for it.

This weekend forced us to stay in and enjoy each other's company with no agenda, and it was wonderful. Yet, despite how much fun it was, it feels so hard to imagine telling people that I'm going to stay in all weekend and watch movies with one person. My mind would be heckled with made-up scenarios about how much I'm disappointing everyone.

That weekend, we had an excuse: we were quarantined, and had no choice. But that forced break reminded us what really matters in life—rest, connection, vulnerability. Why do we need a *reason* to do what's best for us? To rest more? To spend time with someone who means so much to us? Why do I fall into the trap of people pleasing over and over? And how do I get out of that trap—without having to catch COVID-19 every time I need a weekend in?

The answer, turns out, is pretty simple: focus more on what you're doing rather than what others are doing.

Easier said than done, right? We've all heard it said that comparison is the thief of joy. We spend so much of our lives analyzing and feeling behind because of what we see other people doing. The truth is, we experience so much less joy when we constantly compare our lives to others. One of the ways we most often do that is online.

## Social Media and Comparison

These days, we don't just compare ourselves to the people we come face to face with, but with millions every day on social media. Like you read before, falling in love with ourselves means getting to know ourselves. And getting to know ourselves allows us to *be* ourselves in every scenario. In life and online, we can be our true selves. Freedom awaits.

So, how do we practically focus more on what we're doing rather than what others are doing? The first step is to spend less time on social media. I know, I know, you expected this advice. But hear me out: social media is not all bad. According to the Pew Research center's study on "Connection, Creativity and Drama: Teen Life on Social Media in 2022," the majority of teens say social media provides them with a space for connection, creativity, and support. Just like one of my students said in their anonymous letter, "Phones aren't the cause of everything bad, and just because you didn't grow up with as much technology doesn't mean you're better than us."

But according to the same Pew survey, teen girls are more likely than teen boys to say social media has made them feel overwhelmed by drama, excluded by friends, or worse about their life. In fact the Pew survey goes on to show that, "45% of girls say they feel overwhelmed because of all the drama on social media."

One of my students put it this way: "The word is kind of chaotic right now. That added stress of social media makes normal activities harder."

With a simple "delete" button, we can literally "delete" people out of our group chats and lives. And all of us are living in that ruthless environment today.

Not only is exclusion an issue, but we are so connected that we know people's whereabouts at all times. If you think about it, knowing what everyone's doing all of the time isn't natural.

We are each one person living in a community where we now interact with millions of people a day. I don't know when we decided that we needed to be available and reachable at all times. But it is changing us to be humans of comparison, not human *beings.*

We are allowed to take hours and days and weeks off. We are allowed to rest. We are allowed to be fully present. We have full permission to only respond when we are ready. We are not "on-call" workers that need to be slaves to our devices at all times.

How do we fight this constant race? Less hustle, more rest. Less busyness, more peace. Less comparison, more presence. In his book *To Hell with the Hustle,* Christian author Jefferson Bethke puts it this way: "What's my actual goal in life? What am I trying to do here? Keep my head down. Love those in front of me and around me. Honor the process and the present. And be face to face with my Father when I die and hear, *Well done, my good and faithful servant.* Not, *Well accomplished, my busy and hustled servant.* Well done. Faithful."[14]

So, I'm asking you, what is your actual goal in life? Is it to constantly watch what other people are doing online, or is it to make a difference where your feet are, to be present with those in your day-to-day life, to leave a mark on your community?

---

14  Jefferson Bethke, To Hell with the Hustle: Reclaiming Your Life in an Overworked, Overspent, and Overconnected World (Nashville, TN: Nelson Books, an imprint of Thomas Nelson Publishing, 2019), 183.

I am not the golden prize winner for being off of social media, but here are some of my habits that you could try out to live a bit more in the present.

1. Mornings without my phone are my saving grace. In college, I would charge my phone in the other room, use an alarm clock, and go through my morning routine without even checking my phone. Now, I delete my social media apps before going to bed so that I'm not tempted to scroll in the mornings. Am I perfect at this? No. But it's a noble goal.

2. I delete Instagram from my phone for a few days when I feel overwhelmed. I find when I'm not tempted to scroll, I'm so much more pleasant and present in my day.

3. I spend weekends off of social media or off my phone completely, if I can. Better yet, find someone to do this with you—together, put your phones in airplane mode for the weekend and be present.

4. I have found places and people in my life that allow me to be fully present. For example, camp.

Camp has always been a place where I could be fully present. I grew up going to an all-girls camp in Brevard, NC, for a few weeks every summer - where I could completely turn off any expectations and be my true self. I am so thankful that I had a place every summer where I could come as I am, whether I was a nervous elementary schooler, an awkward teenager with braces, or a college student finding my way in the world. Every summer, the heavenly world embraced me and let me be fully present, without technology or social media.

This summer, when I took a group of high schoolers to Young Life Camp in Canada, we took their phones from them at the beginning of the week. There was lots of grumbling and complaining; I mean, how were they going to survive for a whole week off of TikTok? They were going to lose all their Snap streaks! At the end of the week, however, one of my campers came up to me in tears.

"It's perfect here. I don't want to go home. I don't even want my phone back. I don't want to worry about what other people are doing or what parties are going on or worry about what I'm going to wear. I just want to stay here forever."

A place that allows you to be fully present is a beautiful gift.

Not everyone has a place like this, but you may have a person who makes you feel fully content in the present. Your time with Jesus may allow you to forget the outside world. Maybe taking a walk in your neighborhood puts your mind at ease, even for a moment.

What could our lives look like if we spent a little less time online and more time where we are? Less time worrying about others and more time taking care of ourselves? Less time pleasing other people but living a life brimming with love for other people? Think about the possibilities - the lives you could touch, the change you could make, the peace you could have. The joy that would abound from your very being. That seems worth it to me.

People pleasing and comparison are the thieves of joy, and whether we resort to these tendencies in person or online, they are stealing our peace. There are opportunities every day to choose between two paths: living in fear of people's opinions or living in spite of people's opinions.

I pray and hope you choose the latter, fight the people-pleaser tendency, and bask in a life of joy on the other side.

## *JOURNAL IT OUT:*

- Where do you see yourself people-pleasing in life? With your friends, family, or outer circle? Why?
- What is one way you could spend less time on social media? How will you implement that this week?
- Where do you feel most present?

# Chapter 10:
# Accept Love

Life has some big transitions in store for young people—going to college, parents' divorce, and getting married, to name a few. Other seasons of youth, however, can feel a bit mundane—like when you have three years of school left, or are waiting on the acceptance letter or job offer. When you think about it, though, even in these duller moments, we are always in transition. We always think about what's next, yearning for and idealizing the future. When I was in high school, I wanted to be traveling to South America, actualizing my dream. When I was in college, I wanted a full-time job. When I had a job, I wanted a boyfriend. When I got a boyfriend, I wanted to be engaged.

Will the race ever end?

Throughout this book, I've written about my journey of finding joy in life's changes through sharing my mistakes, stories, tidbits of wisdom, and revelations. I have shared with you my advice: to live in community, have a routine, try something new, and appreciate the little things. All these steps will bring you joy in times of change, but the truth is, they might fail you from time to time. The biggest secret to true joy that I've found is *acceptance*.

On a Thursday evening in March, one of my favorite authors and speakers, Annie F. Downs, was coming into town. Seattle was her first show on the west coast ever, and it felt like a special moment that I couldn't miss. I splurged and bought VIP tickets for myself months before, which came with a private Q&A and meet and greet. It was pretty surreal seeing her in person for the first time, a voice I've heard in my car, shower, and while I went on many walks during 2020.

During the Q&A, we wrote down questions for Annie and she answered each of them one by one out loud. In the hurry of the moment, I couldn't think of anything to write, so I scribbled, "How can I find joy in my journey?" This had been the question guiding this whole book—and it had been guiding that entire year for me. Little did I know that when she answered the questions, she would say each of our names and look us straight in the eyes while talking. My face turned bright red when she read my question out loud. My thoughts immediately traveled to, *What is everyone else thinking about me right now? Do they assume I'm going through something hard and can't find joy? Does Annie think I'm depressed?* I felt vulnerable and exposed in a room full of strangers.

Fittingly, when Annie answered my question, she talked about vulnerability. She talked about letting other people in, leaning on other people's hope when you can't, and creating light in the darkness. She talked about the little moments, the little things that bring you joy. She talked about many things that I have written on these pages. Most powerfully, she said, "Joy is accepting where you are and being who you were made to be—a loved and cherished child of God."

From the way the other audience members were locked in on her answer and the sincerity in her voice, I knew this book was needed. She later brought up my question in the live show with over 200 audience guests. I was blown away. I felt God speaking to me over and over that night, saying, "People need to hear about joy. Badly. And you are the one to tell it."

Many times throughout my day as a full-time teacher, I doubted why I was spending any time writing a book. When I said no to social events so I could write, I wondered if this book would amount to anything. But right when the words flowed, I knew that this was what I was made for. Writing is vulnerable, and yet vulnerability—as Annie said—is what leads us to joy. Joy is accepting where and who you are. And while things like routine and hobbies help us get there, *acceptance* is what will push us over the top. We must learn to accept that we are loved, that we are who we are, that we are worthy of joy.

When I was in college, my friends invited me to Grace Church, where they went every Sunday. Although I grew up believing in God, I never fully understood the word "grace." After months of attending, a pastor asked me, "Imagine you just arrived in heaven and met Jesus. What would you tell Him to prove that you could get in?"

I paused for a moment and stumbled over my words, "Um...I would tell Him that I've lived a pretty good life. I've tried my best. I mean, I haven't been perfect, but I've tried my best to follow Him."

The pastor lovingly continued, "You know, the only thing you would need to do is believe in Him."

I started crying. *Grace* is undeserved kindness. Simply receiving love. Letting love change us. Abiding. Rest. It felt too simple, but it felt so true. For the first time, I understood the Gospel.

*Acceptance.*

I usually go to Jesus and just tell Him all my problems so He can tell me what to do. Sometimes, however, I sit with the words He already gave us, and He does something deeper in my heart: He makes me more like Him. He softens my heart without me even asking. He makes me more gentle and kind, and He forgives me. The process of becoming more like Jesus is painful at times. And it doesn't solve our problems. It's not something we do in our own strength. But that's where true joy is found: when we start letting ourselves change, not always trying to change our circumstances to best suit who we currently are.

During my sophomore year of college, during my parents' unexpected divorce, I felt some of the deepest joy I had felt in a long time. I felt so close to Jesus; I was telling everyone about what He's done for me. He loved me, received me, and made me whole. Walking into my sophomore dorm room, I commented to my roommate, "I feel like I have the biggest, most life-changing news to share with everyone. I am *welling up* with joy. I don't even know what to do with it."

# Accept Love

In the darkest season of my life, I felt an intense joy that I haven't felt fully since that moment. Why is that?

As it turns out, some of the writers in the New Testament were writing about being full of God's love and joy while in prison cells, a few while facing execution. So many people in the Bible were going through trials and yet praising God in the midst of hard things. God doesn't promise us an easy life, but He promises to be with us every step of the way.

## Accepting Our Stories

Hannah Brencher says in another Daily Advent Devotional, "I want to say it was not my joy but a supernatural joy God had planted in my spirit to experience within the struggle. Would I maybe change some things or alter the story? Sure, at first glance, yes. But I know the story will never be perfect. And I know the struggle is always going to be a reality."[15]

At first glance, I would also probably change some things about my story. But I also know that because of my story, I am who I am. I have experienced great joy in the struggle. The struggle made my joy more abundant—or maybe, God gave me a deeper joy to make it through my hardship.

Did *I* do something to receive this joy? Do seeds need to *do* anything to become flowers? I didn't become more religious. My routine, my straight As, my adventures, and my hobbies didn't fix me. I didn't wake up one day and decide, "I'm going to feel

---

15  Hannah Brencher, "When Miracles Hurt." Daily Advent Devotional. December 20, 2022. https://www.hannahbrenchercreative.com/advent

101

more joy today." I didn't hunker down and white-knuckle my way to find more joy. I didn't force it.

I accepted. I abided. I let myself be loved. I sat with God, I listened to His gentle voice, and I let Him change me. As I spent more time with God, I learned more about who I was. Who we all are: loved. Cherished. Complete. Worthy.

This is magic. This is the light in my story, in the fear and struggle, I let love envelop me, embrace me—and doing this changed my entire being. This was when I acknowledged, "I'm okay here, too." And I really, really am.

No matter what darkness, hardship, or change will come tomorrow or a year from now, I'll be okay there, too, in the warm embrace of Love.

And so will you.

## JOURNAL IT OUT:

- Write about a time when you made it through something hard, but then realized that you were still okay. What did you feel before, in the middle, and after?
- Why or why not is it hard for you to receive God's love?
- Write a prayer to God, asking for His joy and love in your life

# Bibliography:

The author assumes no responsibility or liability for any errors or omissions in the content of this bibliography.

Chapter 2:

1. Niequist, Shauna. "Waiting for Daylight." *I Guess I Haven't Learned That Yet: Discovering New Ways of Living When the Old Ways Stop Working*, 55. Grand Rapids, MI: Zondervan, 2022.

Chapter 5:

2. Weissbourd, Richard, Milena Batanova, Eric Torres, and Virginia Lovison. "Loneliness in America: How the Pandemic Has Deepened an Epidemic of Loneliness and What We Can Do About It." *Making Caring Common*, February 2021. https://mcc.gse.harvard.edu/reports/loneliness-in-america.

3. Czeisler, Mark É., Rashon I. Lane, Emiko Petrosky, Joshua F. Wiley, Aleta Christensen, Rashid Njai, Matthew D. Weaver, et al. "Mental Health, Substance Use, and Suicidal Ideation during the COVID-19 Pandemic — United States, June 24–30, 2020." *MMWR*.

4. "Supportive Relationships and Active Skill-Building Strengthen the Foundations of Resilience: Working Paper No. 13." National Scientific Council on the Developing Child, March 2015. www.developingchild. harvard.edu.

Chapter 6:

5. Brencher, Hannah. "No Random Days." Daily Advent Devotional. December 1, 2022. https://www.hannahbrenchercreative.com/advent (accessed December 1, 2022).

Chapter 8:

6. Acuff, Jonathan. *Soundtracks: The Surprising Solution to Overthinking,* 22,25. Grand Rapids, MI: Baker Books, a Division of Baker Publishing Group, 2021.

Chapter 9:

7. Bethke, Jefferson. *To Hell with the Hustle: Reclaiming Your Life in an Overworked, Overspent, and Overconnected World,* 183. Nashville, TN: Nelson Books, an imprint of Thomas Nelson Publishing, 2019.

Chapter 10:

8. Brencher, Hannah. "When Miracles Hurt." Daily Advent Devotional. December 20, 2022.https://www.hannahbrenchercreative.com/advent (accessed December 20, 2022)

# Acknowledgments:

My family: Mom, Dad, Whid, and Joe. I am who I am today because of your love and support. While our story hasn't been perfect, I am grateful to have family members that I don't just love, but I like too. I have learned so much from each of you and have grown up surrounded by endless support and love. Thank you for everything.

Brian: Our love is something I will never take for granted. Our partnership is built on trust, honesty, and commitment. From the day I mentioned writing a book, you have encouraged me, read my words, talked me out of my negative self thinking, and supported me. Thank you for your unconditional love.

College friends: The seven of you embody what friendship is to me. I will never take for granted the deep bond we have and the never-ending life we get to do together, even if we're all scattered across the country. Even miles away, I feel your prayers, love, and encouragement immensely. When I think about finding joy in the little moments, walking through hard things in community, and learning to receive love, I think of you all. You are each an inspiration to me in every way.

High school friends: What a privilege and blessing that I got to grow up with some of the most incredible, badass women in the entire world. Even throughout life's changing seasons - break ups, first jobs, moving to a new city, I have gotten to do all of it with all of you just a phone call away. You all have taught me how to fall in love with myself over and over and over. Thank you.

Maggie D: It is rare to say that the girl next door I've known since birth is still one of my best friends. Your adventurous, spontaneous, never willing to settle heart inspires me daily. Ever since we were little girls, I have admired your independence and carefree attitude that has taught me so much. Thank you for bringing me out of my comfort zone and reminding me that life is too short to worry so much.

Abbie, Courtney, and Kat: My Seattle family. You three are the clearest example of God's faithfulness in my life. After we all spent months praying for deep friendship in a new city, He intertwined our paths by all of us living in the same neighborhood. Your willingness to drop what you are doing to help me, encourage me in my dreams, and pray for me has forever changed me.

My Bellevue Young Life community: Your hearts towards kids makes me a better follower of Jesus. I am constantly inspired and in awe of the people I get to surround myself with and do ministry with. Let's keep doing this together - it matters deeply.

Brett: My Self Publishing School Coach. I cannot say enough thank yous for how you have been there every step of the way. It is safe to say that this book wouldn't exist without your guidance, support, encouragement, and time. You are the best of the best. Thank you for making my dream a reality!

Self Publishing School Community: You are all a bunch of world changers! Thank you for being in this book publishing world with me and encouraging me with each of your stories along the way.

Christina, Wandering Words Media: Thank you for editing my book and being a voice of encouragement! Your work is magic, and this book felt even more "me" when you were done with it.

Devon, deproofreading@gmail.com: The best proofreader out there! Thank you for catching all of my mistakes and being so encouraging throughout the process.

My launch team: WE DID IT! Thank you to every one of you who wanted to be a part of this in small and big ways. More people get to hear about finding joy in life because of you all.

My students: I love what I do every single day, and that is because of each of you. Thank you for bringing such joy to my daily life. This book is for you.

My Young Life girls, new and old: Thank you for letting me do life with each of you! I know I'm supposed to be mentoring you, but I learn way more from y'all than you ever could from me. Thank you for being a huge reason I wrote this book. I love each of you.

To every family member, friend, acquaintance, and stranger that has asked about my book, sent an encouraging text, or commented on my Instagram post. Thank you for being a part of my story.

# *URGENT PLEA!*

**Thank You For Reading My Book!**

**I really appreciate all of your feedback and**

**I love hearing what you have to say.**

**I need your input to make the next version of this**

**book and my future books better.**

**Please take two minutes now to leave a helpful review on**

**Amazon letting me know what you thought of the book**

**Thanks so much!**

- Smith

Ready to connect with like minded women who are also looking for ways to live joyfully? Need weekly inspiration to further navigate the changes in your life? Here are your next steps!

Follow me on instagram to join our community of joyful livers!

SMITH_CHILDS

Fill out the form below to stay up to date with allll the things and for weekly inspiration in my newsletter - no spam, only good content to help YOU navigate change in your life!

**https://tinyurl.com/EYSnews**

Want me to come speak at your church, school, or next event about young women navigating change? I would be honored! I love working with groups to help each person navigate life's changes and better benefit the group. I am available for high school assemblies, campus lectures, church events, ministry events, conferences, workshops, and student leadership trainings. Please email smithminard@gmail.com and let us know more about your event and how I could serve you.

Self-Publishing School

NOW IT'S YOUR TURN

Discover the EXACT 3-step blueprint you need to become a bestselling author in as little as 3 months.

Self-Publishing School helped me, and now I want them to help you with this FREE resource to begin outlining your book!

Even if you're busy, bad at writing, or don't know where to start, you CAN write a bestseller and build your best life.

With tools and experience across a variety of niches and professions, Self-Publishing School is the only resource you need to take your book to the finish line!

## DON'T WAIT

Say "YES" to becoming a bestseller:

Made in the USA
Columbia, SC
20 September 2023